No teeth, but lovely gums!

Why the first Alkire Foster Multi-Dimensional Poverty Index
for South Africa was wrong (and the second not much better)

Charles Meth

Published in the United Kingdom by:

Samland Press
Crookes, Sheffield
South Yorkshire
www.povertyand inequality.org

British Library Cataloguing in Publication Data
A catalogue record for this book is available from the British Library

First printed December 2012

Printed by Dolman Scott
www.dolmanscott.com

ISBN 978-0-9575202-0-2

An official portrait of the Rainbow Nation, November 2011

"Statistical indicators paint a disturbing picture of rising violence, increasing numbers of low-income households and other social determinants requiring urgent attention. Among these social concerns are heightened levels of addiction, increasing criminality among young people, high levels of gang-related violence in schools and communities, and sexual violence against women and children, especially in economically deprived areas. Demographic trends and human development indicators point to a country with significant levels of social fragmentation, unacceptable levels of social alienation and the breakdown of social institutions. In the absence of fully functioning families, households, communities and neighbourhoods, social welfare institutions in most countries step in to provide services to improve social functioning and integration.

The combination of poor and inadequate state social welfare services and high levels of poverty and inequality produces social problems and high-risk behaviour that undermines human development and social cohesion. High levels of domestic violence are often amplified by poverty and unemployment. Alcohol abuse is another factor that is both cause and manifestation of stresses in households and communities. Poor social services and ineffective policing reinforce the sense of powerlessness in poor communities. Poor-quality education limits social mobility, further straining basic social relations that many societies take for granted. The impact of youth unemployment and HIV/AIDS has worsened matters." (South Africa: National Planning Commission, NPC, 2011, pp.366-367).

'Paradise found' in danger of becoming 'Paradise lost'

A word picture by an eminent political commentator, a couple of months after the Marikana massacre, in response to rejection of a call by President Zuma for an executive 'wage' freeze

The lived reality of our people is not a liar. It is for this reason that I am now, more than ever, convinced that the social, political and economic veld fires I have been warning about will be upon us much sooner than we think or desire.

If the responses to the executive salary and bonus freeze and the decision itself are anything to go by, South Africa is inexorably sliding towards social, class, racial and economic conflict because we refuse to tell the whole truth about what is wrong about our post-apartheid reality. We seem to think that self-serving political and economic analyses and the fact that we mumble when money talks will alter the truth about inequality, poverty and unemployment in this country.

We are wrong.

We can rearrange the facts or make statistics say things they are not telling us to bolster our argument, but this is not going to change the truth about the lived reality of those South Africans who are being devoured by the wild dogs of unemployment, poverty and inequality. Nor is it going to change what they believe to be true about the real causes of their conditions of underdevelopment.

Their socioeconomic conditions speak the truth more eloquently and more honestly than the selective truths of political and business elites and their apologists. Because their socioeconomic conditions do not lie, I am certain that, every morning, we wake up to the possibility of another Marikana-like Black Swan scenario.

And you can call me an alarmist all you like, or pretend that this column is further evidence of how clueless the middle class is about the social, political and economic realities of our post-apartheid condition, but South Africa will burn if we do not stop lying to our people and ourselves. South Africa will explode if we do not change our ways of seeing and thinking about the future of our country. Therefore, there must come a time when we start admitting to ourselves and to one another that our ways of seeing — to the extent that they are selective, self-serving and are shaped by selfish interest — will turn the South African story to that of a paradise found and lost. We must, therefore, admit that a lot of what we think, say and do about our problems is not sustainable.

Extract from the Opinion piece: "Pacts will not cover up the truth on SA's lived reality" by Aubrey Matshiqi, *Business Day*, 22 October 2012.

Contents

Index of tables

Index of figures

Abstract

Sabina Alkire, of the Oxford Poverty & Human Development Initiative (OPHI) and James Foster have developed a decomposable multi-dimensional poverty index (MPI). Claimed to be 'policy relevant', one version, purportedly measuring 'capabilities' in three 'dimensions' (education, health, living standards), forms the basis for an international league table covering 104 countries. First published by Alkire and Santos, the table is reproduced in the UNDP's *2010 Human Development Report* (HDR).

Mismatches between MPI and income poverty headcount rates occurred in several countries. For South Africa, the MPI rate for 2003 was 3%. – at the $1.25/day line it was 26%.

The 2011 HDR presents a 2008 MPI based on different survey data. The $1.25/day rate falls to 17.4% and the MPI rate rises to 13.4%. Although more plausible, the 2008 MPI still under-estimates the extent of multiple deprivation in South Africa. No message in the 2011 HDR warns users the 2003 MPI is fragile, an uncomfortable truth Alkire and co-workers tried to mitigate by describing it as a 'lower bound' figure.

Errors in the MPI are caused by the use of inappropriate indicators (partly because of data constraints) to measure deprivation in education and health.

The authors fail to detect the South African educational crisis (80% of schools are said to be dysfunctional), and multiple crises in the health sector, especially the devastating HIV/AIDS epidemic. Both affect poor people severely. A simulation exercise suggests the 2008 MPI overlooks somewhere between three and seven million income-poor people experiencing multiple deprivation because of HIV/AIDS.

An appendix glances at the relative inability of poverty statistics to influence policy in the UK and USA.

Take-home message (pardon the lapses into jargon)

Constructing indices is hard work, as everyone who dabbles in the field knows. As soon as one strays beyond uni-dimensional (single variable) indices (and even those are far from being a cake-walk), the hard stuff starts – which indicators to use, how to treat ordinal variables, what weights different components ought to have – and that is just the beginning. Implied trade-offs (what is the going rate for dung floors or living by candle-light, expressed in terms of children's deaths?) are intensely political (and personal). There is clearly something wrong when academics, who do not have to take responsibility for things they say or prescribe, specify the exchange rate. Anyway, once the thing has been designed (also no easy matter, as the amount of axiomatic huffing and puffing by Alkire *et al* testifies), it has to be populated with data. Often, this will come from official statistics, either from surveys and censuses conducted by national statistical services, or administrative data created by governments. Other major sources include universities, international institutions and NGOs.

Surveys on which MPIs rely for data are not designed with the thought in mind that a group of researchers will one day come along, expressing a desire to create an index with this or that marvellous property. Like other researchers, Alkire and her co-workers have to be grateful for what is available. By their own admission, more and better surveys are required, something we have all said at one time or another.

In the case of the South African MPI, the indicators selected to throw light on health and education matters (together, two-thirds of the weight of the MPI) are not 'fit for purpose', to use the jargon. One of the most important requirements of a composite index (indeed, of any index) is that in stripping reality down to bare bones, it 'isolates that reality with maximum clarity'. Both the 2003 and the 2008 MPIs fail this test, being unable to detect signs of major crises in health and education – crises with substantial effects on deprivation levels. The 2003 results for the country are garbage – the first sign of which is the unbelievably large mismatch between income poverty estimates and the MPI. Observing this, Alkire *et al* attempted to negotiate their way around the obstacle by declaring the MPI to be a 'lower bound', a measure as useful (as some say), as a chocolate teapot.

With any luck, no notice will be taken of the South African MPI, except by bad-tempered former intellectuals like myself. Were some addle-pated, rubber-armed ANC politician to pick up the 2003 MPI, one can imagine them trying to pat themselves on the back for all it suggests government has achieved. In the face though, of widespread recognition by government itself of the dire state of health and education for the poor, the hollow reverberations of their contortions would soon fade away. How addle-pate would respond to the apparent deterioration between 2003 and 2008 is not obvious.

Trying to pass off estimates of the 'value' of bog-standard welfare 'dimensions' of health, education and standard of living, as measurements of 'capabilities', creates the impression that Alkire *et al* wish to declare the debate on the measurability of this will-o-the-wisp a settled matter. It is not.

Acknowledgements

It is customary to issue a disclaimer acknowledging that despite the best efforts of colleagues, friends, enemies, editors and the like, the piece of work in question does (or could) still contain errors, the responsibility for which rests solely upon the author. Before naming these folk, let me thank the *Daily Dispatch* newspaper and the *South African Medical Journal* for permission to reproduce the photograph below. As to the manuscript itself, three people read all or parts of the first draft (the final version is draft number 8), Debbie Budlender, Deborah Johnston and Philip White. Their comments are gratefully acknowledged – obviously, they are not to blame for anything that follows. Anna McCord, my partner, has been encouraging, but I have not attempted to push the burden of reading it onto her. Particular thanks are due to Dr Johnston, who invited me to submit a paper drawn from work to the organisers of the 2012 ASAUK conference in Leeds in 2012. Thanks are also due to participants in two seminars at which bits of the thing, in differing vintages, were presented. The first, in October 2011, was to staff and post-graduate students in the School of Environment and Development in the University of Manchester. The other, in March 2012 was to a small audience in the University of Sheffield as part of the SIDnet (Sheffield International Development Network) seminar series. No paper was distributed at either meeting.

In a very real sense, therefore, the errors are mine. No-one else has read this final draft (nor the second, third, fourth, fifth, sixth or seventh), with its hundreds upon hundreds of 'facts', references, citations, estimates, opinions, simulations, speculations, guesses and what have you. I have been as careful as I could, but it is inevitable that 'they' (typographical errors, conceptual errors, errors of calculation and of citation) will have sneaked through. Peer review would get rid of most of them, and a good editor, the rest – it's a pity the manuscript did not enjoy those luxuries (a sentiment certain to be endorsed, even if the reader who does so does not agree with anything else in the text). While there are likely to be errors in subsidiary arguments, the central claim, I hope, will prove able to withstand challenge. Readers, should there be any, who discover errors will earn my gratitude (possibly) if they advise me of them by writing to chasmeth@gmail.com.

There is a certain urgency (at least for me) about placing this thing in the public domain, so, apart from the deposit library copies, it is to be published electronically – I lack both the time and the resources to travel down the formal academic pathway. Besides, it contains a few fruity expressions and other indulgences that are unlikely to survive editorial disapproval. To those who condemn 'vanity self-publishing' with patronising curl of lip, the consolation of peer-reviewed, economic research, much of it over-mathematised and/or wholly irrelevant, is available in abundance – enjoy.

Stop Press

In November 2012, the fruits of an 18-month collaboration between Demos and Natcen, with help from the Esmée Fairbairn Foundation, were published (Wood *et al*, 2012). The project's goal was 'to create a new model for understanding poverty in a multi-dimensional way.' Crucially, the project does not seek to redefine poverty – rather, it takes an existing measure of income poverty, then seeks to discover how many forms of deprivation are suffered by various categories of people in the low income group netted by the income measure. Unlike Alkire and her colleagues, Demos and Natcen do not seek to aggregate these deprivations into a single (decomposable or not) measure. They explicitly reject the Alkire Foster (AF) methodology thus:

> "In our analysis we have not followed the model of multidimensional poverty developed by Sabina Alkire and James Foster at the Oxford Poverty and Human Development Initiative, which counts the number of dimensions of disadvantage experienced by a household, and deems all households that experience above a certain number to be poor. All of the households in our sample are deemed to be poor by dint of their low income, but knowing the number of dimensions likely to be faced by different groups (pensioners as opposed to families, for example) helps us to understand the nature of their poverty experience." (Wood *et al*, 2012, pp.177-178)

Using vastly superior data-bases to those that generated the MPIs published by the UNDP, Wood *et al* dig deeply into poverty experiences to identify distinct groups (15 of them) suffering similar sets of deprivations. An approach such as this, is of obvious use to policy-makers (it was designed with that purpose in mind).

The Alkire Foster approach, with its aim of being able to 'target the poorest groups', could be modified to do something similar, but only at the cost of scrapping the contentious process of indicator weighting and cut-off point selection necessary to identify and count the 'poorest'. Since the latter features constitute the MPI's claim to fame, the operation could be a success, but the patient would die.

The Wood *et al* (Demos/Natcen) approach cannot be used to create international league tables – any country seeking to apply the method would have to identify its own vulnerable groups and their characteristics. For those given to playing with league tables, the AF MPIs have a certain appeal – whether the numbers offered have any meaning, let alone any relevance for policy, is moot.

Stop Press Again

On the 27th November 2012, the long-awaited official poverty lines for South Africa finally made their appearance. They do not affect the argument at all (sigh of relief!), having minimal impact on the discussion below in section 3 headed "Which poverty lines, if any, can we trust?" Most importantly, they confirm the claims below about the inadequacies of the MPI – a measure that discovers 13 per cent of the population to be suffering multi-dimensional poverty when 26 per cent of the people lack the wherewithal to buy sufficient food, cannot be taken seriously.

Two tables from the Living Conditions Survey of 2008/2009 are reproduced below to show how bad things were. The first of them provides Foster-Greer-Thorbecke income poverty estimates for a number of poverty lines. The second repeats the 'Objective' estimates, then gives a set of 'subjective poverty' estimates generated by the survey. The latter is a multi-dimensional measure covering food consumption, housing, clothing, health care, and children's schooling. To aggregate these dimensions into a single index, Statistics South Africa makes use of the Alkire Foster method, citing a paper of theirs published in 2011 (Alkire, S and Foster, J. "Counting and multidimensional poverty measurement", *Journal of Public Economics*, 2011, Vol. 95, pp.476-487).

Poverty line	Poverty headcount (P_0)	Poverty gap (P_1)	Severity of poverty (P_2)
Food poverty line (R305) per capita per month	26.3	8.5	3.8
Lower-bound poverty line (R416) per capita per month	38.9	15.0	7.5
Upper-bound poverty line (R577) per capita per month	52.3	23.6	13.3
$1.25 (PPP) per capita per day	10.7	2.8	1.1
$2.50 (PPP) per capita per day	36.4	13.5	6.7

Source: *Living Conditions Survey 2008/09: Poverty Profile of South Africa, Application of the poverty lines on the LCS 2008/2009*, Report No. 03-10-03 (2008/2009), Pretoria: Statistics South Africa, 27 November 2012, p.6.

The income poverty headcount rate lies between 39 and 53 per cent, while the subjective multi-dimensional poverty headcount rate lies between 39 and 59 per cent, depending on the method used to estimate it. Of course, as Alkire and Foster point out, different MPIs measure different aspects of poverty – they are allegedly measuring 'acute poverty'. As noted above though, it is a very peculiar measure that refuses to recognise that existing below the food poverty line does not constitute serious deprivation.

Poverty line	Individuals	Households
Objective poverty (%)		
Food poverty line (R305 per person per month)	26.3	16.2
Lower-bound poverty line (R416 per person per month)	38.9	26.0
Upper-bound poverty line (R577 per person per month)	52.3	38.0
Subjective poverty (%)		
Self-perceived wealth question (SPWQ)	39.5	37.7
Minimum income question (MIQ)	55.3	56.2
Income evaluation question (IEQ)	58.6	56.7

Source: *Subjective Poverty in South Africa: Findings of the Living Conditions Survey 2008/09*, Report No. 03-10-01 (2008/2009), Pretoria: Statistics South Africa, 27 November 2012, p.21.

Abbreviations

AF	Alkire Foster
AIDS	Acquired immune deficiency syndrome
ANC	African National Congress
ART	Anti-retroviral treatment
ARV	Anti-retro viral
ASAUK	African Studies Association of the UK
ASSA	Actuarial Society of South Africa
CASASP	Centre for the Analysis of South African Social Policy
BHPS	British Household Panel Survey
BPL	Below the Poverty Line (India)
CDF	Cumulative distribution function
CD4	Cluster of differentiation 4
CPAG	Child Poverty Action Group
CMP	Capabilities Measurement Project
CS	Community Survey
DA	Democratic Alliance
DfWP	Department for Work and Pensions (UK)
DfE	Department for Education (UK)
DHS	Demographic and Health Survey
DBSA	Development Bank of Southern Africa
FGT	Foster Greer and Thorbecke
GGP	Gross Geographic Product
GII	Gender Inequality Index
GNP	Gross National Product
HAART	Highly active anti-retroviral treatment
HDI	Human Development Index
HDR	Human Development Report
HIV	Human immunodeficiency virus
HPI	Human Poverty Index
HSRC	Human Sciences Research Council
ICU	Intensive care unit
IMD	Index of Multiple Deprivation
IES	Income and Expenditure Survey
IFS	Institute for Fiscal Studies
LCS	Living Conditions Survey
MSc	Master of Science
MDG	Millennium Development Goals
MRD	Ministry of Rural Development (India)
MRT	Multi-drug resistant type (TB)
MPI	Multi-Dimensional Poverty Index
NGO	Non-governmental organisation
NDP	National Development Plan
NEET	Not in employment, education or training
NFHS	National Family Health Survey (India)

NHDR	National Human Development Report
NPC	National Planning Commission
OECD	Organisation for Economic Co-operation and Development
OPHI	Oxford Poverty & Human Development Initiative
PIMD	Provincial Indices of Multiple Deprivation
PIRL	Progress in International Reading Literacy Study
PLWH	People living with HIV/AIDS
PPE	Politics, Philosophy and Economics
PPP	Purchasing Power Parity
PSLSD	Project for Statistics on Living Standards and Development
SADHS	South African Demographic and Health Survey
Saldru	Southern African Labour and Development Research Unit
SANAC	South African National AIDS Council
SAQMEC	Southern and East African Consortium for Monitoring Educational Quality
SDRC	Social Disadvantage Research Centre
SES	Socio-Economic Status
Stats SA	Statistics South Africa
STI	Sexually transmitted infection
TB	Tuberculosis
TIMMS	Trends in International Mathematics and Science Studies
UK	United Kingdom
UNDP	United Nations Development Programme
USA	United States of America
WHO	World Health Organization
WHR	World Health Report
WHS	World Health Survey
YPLL	Years of Potential Life Lost

"A statistician is a person with one foot in boiling water and one foot in freezing water who declares that on the average he's comfortable." Attributed to Mark Twain by Disraeli(?)

"We need to keep an open mind, but not so open that our brains drop out." (Eddie Webster)

"When all else fails, lower your standards." (Anon)

Section 1 Introduction and a first critical bite at the MPI

It is a pity that J P Donleavy, author of *The Unexpurgated Code: A Complete Manual of Survival & Manners,* and other execrable works, having offered sound and detailed advice on how to behave in unfamiliar social settings, did not turn his fertile mind to the compilation of a similar guide for economists (myself not excluded) bent upon inflicting the fruits of their endeavours on a hapless public. Anxious to make good this sad oversight, and filled with public-spiritedness, I wrote an entry for the compendium or encyclopaedia (I am not sure which) of works on the poverty of poverty measurement – it bears title "How not to present poverty research results: The South African case" (Meth, 2011). From the story to be recounted below, it will become clear that on the subject of good manners for economists (once again, my own not excepted), there is much work to be done.

In 2010, an unsuspecting world had foist upon it yet another way (with certain novel features) of showing the extent to which many of its denizens suffered multiple deprivations, amounting to acute poverty. In their anxiety to bring the (often bad) news to the attention of a wide audience, Alkire and Santos (2010a) creators (along with James Foster) of a magic number, the Multiple-deprivation Poverty Index (MPI), rushed into print with an estimate of it for South Africa so obviously silly that anyone with modest knowledge of conditions in that country should have been able, supposing they could disengage their minds from more pressing matters, to dismiss it with the contempt it merited. No such dismissal was forthcoming – to make matters worse, the number was broadcast more widely in the *2010 Human Development Report* (UNDP, 2010). It is only fair to say that my initial reaction to the publication of the MPI was not as polite as that above, *au contraire, mes amis,* an angry THAT'S NOT MY COUNTRY! was followed immediately by the question: 'who is responsible for this nonsense? Must be another one of those (often well-meaning) international experts,[1] everywhere to be found, proclaiming their desire to help the developing develop! How many times have third-worlders had to bite their tongues and listen politely to experts talking rubbish? In South Africa, where an often violent struggle by poor people has been waged to convince the authorities that anti-poverty policies are not working well enough or fast enough, up pops an expert from the better class of university, to inform a government slavering for good news, that things may not be too bad. But soft, this is not the work of some World Bank rent-a-brain – Alkire is one of 'ours' – what is going on?

Readers of this tome, if there be any, may be surprised at the vehemence of my critique of the Alkire and Santos estimates – why, they may ask, is it necessary to go to such lengths? The answer is simple – it is because politicians, especially when they are in a tight corner, abuse statistics. That being so, it behoves researchers to make every effort to ensure that users are aware of the fragilities of their workmanship. Although ultimately, there may be little that can be done to prevent abuse, there are steps that can be taken to minimise the damage done. It will be shown below that Alkire and her colleagues do not live up to the demands this injunction places upon them.

As Alkire *et al* undoubtedly know, poverty (and inequality) estimates are not neutral, objective, value-free products of social science, they are often highly-politicised artifacts. When playing with toys like that, the need for care is multiplied several-fold. If, in addition to being politically sensitive, the estimates in question are flimsy, serious consideration ought to be given to withholding them altogether – as an eminent econometrician once said:

"A fragile inference is not worth taking seriously." (Leamer, 1985)

Distortion of 'reality' in the country of my birth leads to the regurgitation in my mind of a protracted battle to get the authorities to recognise that the use of methodologically unsound, but politically attractive estimates of (income) poverty reduction in South Africa like those made, for example, by Prof. Servaas van der Berg and his colleagues in the University of Stellenbosch, was not a good idea.[2] They fuelled, I would argue, a baseless optimism at the highest political levels that poverty would be halved by 2014 (an MDG goal, brought forward to coincide with

---

[1] Some of the less scrupulous international 'experts' surely merit the description penned by a wag who described them as consultants who have flown over a developing country twice by daylight.

[2] There is a long list in the references section of the present work of the papers I have written on poverty, unemployment and related matters. Almost without exception, they warn against the dangers of the sloppy use of numbers.

the 20th anniversary of democracy in South Africa). Neither that goal, nor the equally optimistic one of halving unemployment by 2014, has any hope of being achieved. Some significant part of my life has been devoted to backing up these claims with evidence – to witness an interloper approaching the subject with less than the caution this important matter requires is distressing, to say the very least. The consequences of the failure to make more progress in the struggle against poverty and unemployment have not been pretty – they are likely to become less so. Acknowledgement of achievement is necessary and desirable – anything, however, that offers the régime an opportunity to lay claim to unearned kudos, is greatly to be deplored.

Be all that as it may, perhaps regretting the folly of premature publication, Alkire and her colleagues provided an amended estimate of the MPI for South Africa, of somewhat greater plausibility (but still incorrect, it will be argued below) for the *2011 Human Development Report* (HDR, 2011). The relevant figures are reproduced below in Table 1. They are on view in the 'Country Briefings' produced by Alkire *et al* (2010b; 2011).

Table 1 The 2003 and 2008 MPIs compared

	Population in multi-dimensional poverty		Population below income poverty line (%)	
	Headcount		PPP $1.25/day	National poverty line
Year	%	1000s		
2003	3.1	1500	26.2	22
2008	13.4	6609	17.4	23
Source: Alkire and Santos, 2010a (p.74) and 2010b; Alkire *et al*, 2011.				

Those without knowledge of the country, reading through the Country Briefings for 2003 and 2008 may be excused for concluding that a dramatic (pardon the hackneyed adjective) deterioration in conditions had taken place in South Africa. Neither of the two briefings offers any explanation for the apparently huge change that takes place between those years. Nor do the 2010 and 2011 *Human Development Reports* offer users specific health warnings about the South African MPI. To find even a lame excuse for the silliness of the 2003 MPI, they would have to journey to the Alkire and Santos 2010a paper, there to discover the recommendation that the MPI headcount for that year be treated as a 'lower bound'.

Presented with results for 2003 that suggest that while $1.25/day poverty is still unacceptably high (a headcount ratio of 26 per cent), improvements in health, education and economic wellbeing leave only three per cent of the population suffering acute multiple deprivation, what conclusions could have been drawn by the average, not particularly well-informed politician in South Africa (anxious as many are to be assured that the ANC government has effected significant improvements in the wellbeing of the poor since the official demise of apartheid)? That government's health and education policies (dimensions of the MPI that account for two thirds of its total magnitude), have enjoyed great success? Anyone with an interest in the outcomes of the South African experiment in democracy would know that this is not so, something that even the ANC government, for all its attempts to gloss over its lack of progress in the struggle against income poverty (Meth, 2008; 2011), shows little sign of denying. One can almost imagine a sigh of relief when estimates for 2008 appeared, looking more like the South Africa of years of violent protest against poor service delivery.

A change in data sources is what accounts for the 'improvement' in the quality of the South African MPI – it has brought the 2008 result closer to the reality of the multiple deprivation the index seeks (in highly abstract form) to represent. This notwithstanding, the fundamental flaws that turned the 2003 results into garbage are still present in the 2008 estimates. It is possible that something similar is true for other countries. This is an interesting question but not one that will be explored here – the primary goal of the present paper is to explore the 'fundamental flaws' in the South African estimates.

The paper's structure is as follows:

- Section 1 introduces the MPI's results for South Africa
- Section 2 traces the history of the MPI and looks at a few more of its problems
- Section 3 digs a little deeper into the results it has generated for South Africa
- Section 4 looks briefly at education and poverty in South Africa
- Section 5 does the same for health, but in more depth
- Section 6 attempts a conclusion

At the end of the paper there are two appendices: the first consists of summaries of the challenges in the health and education sectors as seen by the National Planning Commission when it developed its vision for South Africa for the year 2030 (NPC, 2011), while the second peeps into the use of poverty statistics in the UK and USA.

Under the umbrella heading of 'what to expect from a new composite index' this section of the paper attempts to do the following:

- It asks first how one should respond when a survey used to generate an index proves to be inadequate (because too much has been asked of it)
- It then asks what constitutes appropriate criticism of the index
- Probing more deeply, it examines the claims made for the capabilities of the index, then asks whether available data are such as to allow for their realisation
- The section is brought to a close with a discussion of questions raised by the issue of policy relevance – matters, for example, such as error detection and survey choice are considered

The MPI first came to my attention when I was working on the "How not to present poverty research results" paper referred to above. Published by the Southern African Labour and Development Research Unit (Saldru) in the University of Cape Town, the focus of that paper was the weaknesses (in application) of the, by now, standard Foster Greer and Thorbecke (FGT) poverty measures. In the course of a homily on the virtues of not throwing out the baby with the bathwater by neglecting uni-dimensional poverty measures in favour of increasingly fashionable multi-dimensional measures, I commented in a footnote (n.70, p.50) on the huge mismatch between the 2003 MPI and $1.25/day poverty headcount rates (the figures Table 1 above). In a somewhat garbled sentence, I noted that it was an area crying out for further investigation.[3]

After an encouraging reception of my first attempt to come to grips with the MPI,[4] the real work began. It was with some relief that I discovered that a hatchet job on the multi-dimension index industry, couched in the politest terms, had already been attempted by Martin Ravallion (2010; 2011).[5] This elicited a response from Alkire,

---

[3] One of the early fruits of the investigation was the discovery that the 2003 MPI reversed the findings made by Klasen using the 9000-household 1993 Saldru/PSLSD data set. Comparing the headcounts found using the multi-dimensional index he constructed (14 indicators) with those disclosed by the more generous of two expenditure poverty lines, he noted that: "If the deprivation index was indeed the true measure of deprivation, about 17 percent of the 20 million truly deprived are not identified by the expenditure measure." (Klasen, 2000, p.54). Of course, a comparison of their respective results is not valid because the measures used are different. Had it been valid, it would have implied that the ANC government had, in scarcely a decade, been able to resolve most of the problems in the health and education sectors in South Africa, something that rather obviously has not taken place.

[4] At a seminar on 11 October 2011, presented to staff and post-graduate students in the School of Environment and Development in the University of Manchester.

[5] I was guided to the Ravallion papers by the MPI's creators, in a paper by Alkire and Foster called "Understandings and Misunderstandings of Multidimensional Poverty Measurement" (2011).

Foster and Santos (2011). Although the ping-pong of the arguments makes for interesting reading, it is not necessary here to join that particular fray. When I started work in earnest on the present paper (mid-October 2011), my goal was modest – I sought only to try to demonstrate, and to explain why the MPI, in the form it assumed in 2010, had little of the policy relevance claimed for it by Alkire and Santos. All it could do, I argued, was to cause mischief.

Unaware of the major revisions to the South African MPI published in the 2011 *Human Development Report*, I plunged in at the deep end, tracing the 2003 MPI weaknesses to their source in the inability of the indicators used by Alkire *et al* to capture the contribution of inadequate health and education to multiple deprivation. Much of the initial analysis was completed before I looked at the 2011 HDR.[6] Although the 2008 MPI is an improvement on the 2003 estimate, the weaknesses that caused the latter to go so seriously awry, are still present. The analysis stands, therefore, more or less as it did before I discovered the 2008 MPI. The changes required to accommodate it were superficial. The main conclusion reached in earlier versions of the paper, namely, that as it stood (and still stands), the South African MPI has little or no relevance, is unchanged.

Few social scientists, brought face-to-face with a gross mismatch between estimated income poverty levels, and estimated levels of multi-dimensional deprivation in their country could gaze with indifference upon a chasm of great depth – I am certainly not among their number. When digging failed to reveal (a) evidence of suitable warnings about the extreme fragility of the South African MPI, and (b) no satisfactory explanation of the gap, the impulse to explore the thing in depth became irresistible. As noted above, the 'lower bound' caution Alkire and Santos offer is far from satisfactory – it serves only to prompt the question of why any researcher would wish to publish suspect results from a survey too weak to bear the burden imposed upon it (that much is clear from their inability to estimate an upper bound for the MPI). There is abundant (widely-disseminated) evidence of the deprivation suffered by millions of poor people in South Africa in the 'dimensions' of health and education (not all of it qualitative). What animates the present study is a desire to present enough of that evidence to make the point that it can and should be used to

---

[6] Two earlier versions of the present paper make no reference to the 2008 MPI. Version 1, the first of these, making essentially the same arguments as are to be found in the current version, was circulated to colleagues in various universities on 22nd December 2011. Version 2, incorporating corrections, but with the central arguments unchanged, went out to an expanded list on 31st January 2012. It is as well that I soldiered on without knowing about the 2011 HDR changes – had there been at my disposal only the results for the year 2008, it is possible that my suspicions would not have been aroused to the same extent, thus leaving the fundamental flaws in the MPI undetected.

ensure that highly abstract measures like the MPI do not drift off into Cloud Cuckoo Land (Νεφελοκοκκυγία).[7]

Proper conduct upon discovering one's chosen survey has let one down

The story commences with a simple question, one that requires precious little knowledge of the detailed workings of the MPI. The question is simply this: how should Alkire and Santos have responded upon discovering that the 2003 South African MPI was garbage? The answer offered here has universal applicability – when any purveyor of statistics finds out that they have made an error, the proper thing to do is (a) to warn all users, (b) discuss the possible implications of the error, and (c) describe exactly what they have done to fix it.

Without knowing anything about the way in which the MPI is constructed, a mere glance at the two charts below, each purporting to show the contributions of various indicators to the MPI, would be sufficient to persuade even the most jaded onlooker

---

[7] Apropos absolutely nothing at all, how often does a phrase, a few notes of music, or a whiff, pleasant or otherwise, summon up something from the past, only for the 'memory' to float tantalisingly out of reach? So it was with the cliché 'cloud cuckoo land', once I had typed it. Fortunately, that old and not always trustworthy friend, Wikipedia, was there not only to remind me that it comes from Aristophanes' play *The Birds* (a fine factlet for a game of Trivial Pursuit), but also to bring back to mind Margaret Thatcher's alleged declaration in 1987 that: "The ANC is a typical terrorist organisation ... Anyone who thinks it is going to run the government in South Africa is living in cloud-cuckoo land." (Uttered, of course, in the "calm and authoritative tone", glued, with the assistance of Laurence Olivier (nice one, Baron Olivier!), onto her "too shrill" natural manner of speaking, with its "hectoring tone of the housewife". See the article "How Laurence Olivier gave Margaret Thatcher the voice that went down in history" by Polly Dunbar in *Mail*online, 30th October 2011. Her widely-reported remark, coming as it did on top of her tacit support of the apartheid regime over the years, intensified the dislike she aroused in progressive circles (not that that would have caused her loss of sleep). Although widely reported, the story may be apocryphal. One account traces its origin to her press secretary, Bernard Ingham, who is reported to have said in response to speculation by a Canadian journalist that the ANC might overthrow the white South African regime: "It is cloud-cuckoo-land for anyone to believe that could be done." For the Ingham story, see the correction by Ned Temko printed in *The Observer's* "For the record column", Sunday September 10 2006, to the article "Cameron: we got it wrong on apartheid", in *The Observer*, Sunday 27 August 2006. Ken Livingstone's piece "Mandela's long walk to a plinth", in *The Guardian*, Friday 20 April 2007, repeats the story. For a retelling of the apocryphal tale see The Special Report: Mandela turns 85, "Mandela's triumphant walk", by Donwald Pressly, in NEWS24.com, 18/07/2003. Downloaded from: http://web.archive.org/web/20080112081508/http://www.news24.com/News24/South-Africa/Mandela/0,,2-7-1507_1389526,00.html

that something is amiss. As source for the 2003 MPI, Alkire and Santos used the 2003 World Health Survey (WHS) for South Africa. For the 2008 MPI, the WHS has been booted out in favour of the National Income Dynamics Survey (NIDS), a longitudinal survey conducted by Saldru.

Figure 1 Contributions of indicators to the 2003 MPI

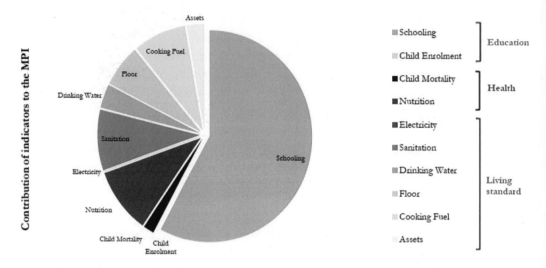

Source: Alkire and Santos, 2010b.

Figure 2 Contributions of indicators to the 2008 MPI

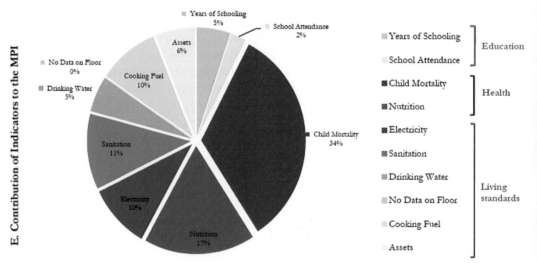

Source: Alkire *et al*, 2011.

'Schooling' (years of schooling) was responsible for almost 60 per cent (57.8) of the 2003 MPI; child mortality for 1.7 per cent of it, and nutrition for 10.0 per cent. For the 2008 MPI, the contribution of years of schooling shrinks to a mere 5.2 per cent; child mortality grows to 33.4 per cent, while the contribution of nutrition (actually, poor nutrition) grow to 17.1 per cent.

Nongazi Sopose, with her son, Bathandwa (4 months), at the graveside of his twin sister Siule, who died of diarrhoeal disease after the Barkly East water system collapsed.

Picture: Nigel Louw, *Daily Dispatch*, in
South African Medical Journal, June 2008, pp.430

When an event of this sort occurs, the rules of polite social intercourse require, as has been pointed out above, that readers be offered an explanation and an apology. Since, as was noted above, neither has been forthcoming, Alkire and her colleagues are guilty of a serious breach of etiquette. Not only that, they are guilty of negligence for not classing as reject, a set of results of such obvious implausibility – that the data are poor is no excuse – if they are so fragile, do not publish the estimate. If Alkire *et al* believe the noise they make about 'policy relevance', then ensuring that the 'country briefings' they distribute are at least consonant with social reality in the country they are 'briefing', should be an unbreakable rule. If, as in the present case, it is broken, users should be advised as soon as possible and offered a proper explanation (not 'the train is late because of operational reasons').

All of which brings us to a discussion of what, apart from relief from the sort of indiscretion discussed above, may reasonably be demanded of a new poverty index.

This includes a consideration of the qualities the MPI would have to possess in order to be considered 'policy relevant'.

What constitutes reasonable criticism of the MPI?

Reasonable criticism of the MPI falls into more than one category – two will be considered here. In the first place, there are errors of the sort addressed immediately above, where corrections are made without drawing them to user's attention. In the second, there are criticisms that need to be made within limits set by the nature of the index itself. We commence with an example of the first type, then dig into the second.

Having uncovered a series of mismatches between MPIs and income poverty measures such as the $1.25/day international line, Alkire and Santos paper paid some attention to the problem of (2010a, pp.41ff), offering tentative explanations (discussed further below),[8] in addition to issuing the 'lower bound' warning. They then blot their copybook by ignoring the warning with the following statement:

> "Africa presents the highest MPI poverty rates, with considerable variation among the 38 countries. The percentage of multidimensionally poor ranges from 3 percent in South Africa to 93 percent in Niger…. " (2010a, p.47)

Of the mismatch story the 2010 HDR gives little warning – the 'lower bound' caveat does not seem to have been repeated outside of the Alkire and Santos 2010a paper. The non-specialist reader, unlikely to consult an academic paper, was given no guidance in the 2010 HDR as to which results needed to be treated with circumspection. The HDR discusses limitations of the MPI (UNDP, 2010, pp.99-100), resulting mainly, the authors suggest, and not unreasonably so, from data constraints. It is silent, however, on the question of which MPI estimates can be trusted.[9] Having had numerous squabbles with the Central Statistical Services (the

---

[8] Some indicators in the MPI apply only to households containing children. If the method used by Alkire and Santos to deal with 'households with non-applicable population' is not satisfactory (2010a, p.26), it is possible that this may explain part of the mismatch between the MPI and income poverty estimates.

[9] In a paper whose purpose it is to elucidate aspects of the MPI, a measure its authors describe as "… quite a departure from traditional unidimensional and multidimensional poverty measurement… " Alkire and Foster (2011), commenting on the estimates for 104 countries made by Alkire and Santos (2010a) that appear in the 2010 HDR, observe that the: "… exercise revealed the applicability of this methodology, and stimulated interest in similar analyses." (2011, p.19) The AF methodology may well deserve this 'interest' – it could have been the case that South African results were so exceptional as to make the

apartheid regime name for what is now known as Statistics South Africa) in the 1980s and early 1990s over the issue of health warnings, it feels weird to be berating an otherwise reputable purveyor of statistics in the year of grace 2012, for not giving proper guidance to users. And so, to the second type of criticism.

If one is to look critically at any instrument, one needs to be careful not to overstep the boundary between relevant and irrelevant charges – only a fool would bemoan the fact that a harpsichord cannot make sounds like a bassoon. The case of the MPI is no exception. A first stipulation is that to make valid criticisms of composite indicators, a clear understanding of the relationship between an index, and the reality from which it is drawn is necessary. Although as a starting point, it may be acceptable to observe, as has been done above, that the MPI little resembles the country whose predicament it is supposed to illuminate, greater precision is required if the criticism is to be sustained.

One source of guidance in this matter may be found in a paper by Gutiérrez *et al* (2011).[10] They are interested in measuring poor state performance. Rather than ranking states as Alkire and her colleagues do, they bring a novel approach to the matter, sorting states into categories (with fuzzy boundaries).[11] Our interest lies not so much in the method they develop as in the methodological chapter with which their paper commences. Although much of it is of relevance, it is not necessary to summarise the chapter here – all that will be taken from it is a guide to a route around a major pitfall, namely, that of damning the MPI for its failure to capture 'context'. They commence with the proposition that:

> "Indexes are supposed to be (extreme) simplifications of reality. The demand that they describe the context or the complex historical trajectory of concrete countries is incorrect. This is the forte of qualitative research and indexes cannot, and should not, try to imitate this. Indexes are powerful precisely because they are (aggressively) simple and shed a substantial amount of context in their calculation."

Abstract indexes cannot capture context – as they note:

---

country an extreme outlier. The possibility also exists, however, that what is true for South Africa, is true for a number of other countries as well.

[10] Thanks are due to Prof Chris Cramer of SOAS, University of London, who, in discussions about the problems of composite indexes, introduced me to the work of Gutiérrez.

[11] Naidoo (2007) has estimated multiple deprivation indices for South Africa for the years 2001 and 2006 using four different methodological approaches. One of them is based on fuzzy logic.

"Even in disciplines where measurement is relatively clear cut, context plays a decisive role. Given that the very nature of index building is abstracting and producing context-free tags (numerical, verbal or any other type), their inability to capture context is an intrinsic limit. Indexes are not designed to take the context (fully) into account." (Gutiérrez *et al*, 2011, p.8)

This notwithstanding, in the process of extracting those aspects of 'reality' that will constitute the index, care has to be taken to ensure that the indicators chosen to 'capture reality' do so adequately. In their words:

"… indexes cannot be attacked because they isolate reality. Rather, this is part of their strength and contribution. The issue of data quality is fundamental but not always insuperable. *What should be demanded of indexes is that they isolate reality with the maximum of clarity*, and squarely address the relevant data problems. Once again, this is easily said and not so easily done." (Gutiérrez *et al*, 2011, p.9, emphasis added)

In the discussions below on education and health in South Africa, it will be shown that in the process of constructing the 2003 MPI, Alkire and Santos (2010a) manage to miss major crises in both sectors. This is NOT a complaint about the failure of the MPI to deliver messages about context; rather it is to point out that it has failed (abysmally) to 'isolate reality with the maximum of clarity'. The Alkire *et al* (2011) estimate of the 2008 MPI suffers from the same weakness, albeit to a lesser degree because of the improved quality of the survey data used.

Another piece of guidance is drawn from the 2011 paper by Alkire and Foster. They seek to prevent critics from falling into paths of unrighteousness and misunderstanding, by drawing attention to five pitfalls that must be avoided. Our interest is in the third of these, which warns against the error of thinking that:

"… the *particular* MPI dimensions, indicators, cutoffs, and weights, are part of the general *methodology*, instead of recognising the range of calibration choices that are possible. The parameters chosen for the international MPI reflect acute poverty across developing countries within strongly binding data constraints; other specifications could be considered – for example to measure national poverty, target beneficiaries, or evaluate a particular intervention." (Alkire and Foster, 2011, p.19, emphasis in original)

This is an important injunction – it needs to be unpacked in order to ensure that compliance does not stifle valid criticism. If a particular dataset generates garbage, as the 2003 World Health Survey (WHS) did when applied to South Africa, then calling those results garbage is not calling the 'general methodology' into question.

If the 'general methodology' enjoys widespread acceptance,[12] then the only sources of error are (i) the 'particular MPI dimensions, indicators, cutoffs, and weights' chosen, and (ii) the data used. That way lies the route to a critique.

Deficiencies in the specification of the 'dimensions, indicators, cutoffs, and weights' for a particular MPI, or in the data used, will result in failure of the measure to achieve what its creators claim it is able to do. The over-arching claim made for the MPI is that it can deliver policy relevant results. Measuring policy relevance is, in most cases, difficult if not impossible. It is however, reasonable to stipulate that 'policy relevant' measures or indicators must be 'accurate' if there is to be any hope of their making a positive contribution to policy formation, implementation, monitoring or evaluation. In the case of the MPI, a finding that one or other of the many forms that the index can take, fails to achieve what it is supposed to, because adequate survey data are not available, does not rule out the possibility that tailor-made surveys may at some point in the future become available, which would enable it to achieve the desired result. Similarly, if, as is argued to be the case in the present paper, failure may be traced to the use of inappropriate indicators, the possibility of more appropriate choices being made at some point in the future must be admitted.

Before setting out on a detailed critique of South Africa's MPI estimates, it is thus important to make it clear that the critique is aimed not at the MPI as an abstract structure (even though composite indices are clearly problematic), but rather at a particular set of MPI estimates. In other words, our concern is with the here and now. This does not preclude speculation about future possibilities of the MPI, as long as it is clear that it is just that – speculation.

Presented with an index that, by assembling data in a novel way, purports to offer policymakers new and convincing insights into the combinations of deprivation that mark off the most acutely deprived, nothing that has been said above would prevent a critic from finding, if it were the case, that the claims could not be sustained.

In the abstract, the Alkire Foster MPI does what it says on the label – their novel way of analysing survey data, at least potentially, offers insights not previously obtainable (it is quite capable of doing so without all the hot air about capabilities). Whether or not it is able to do so in a way that would convince policymakers and the academic community, not to mention the subjects of the data analysis, depends on (a) the indicators selected to measure deprivation, (b) the manner in which they are

---

[12] For an example of the praise showered upon the technical edifice that Alkire and her co-workers have built, see Gordon and Nandy (2012, p.79).

combined into a composite index, and (c) the adequacy of the surveys (or censuses) from which the data required to estimate the value of the MPI are drawn.

Claimed uses of the MPI, and the data required to meet the claims

It is possible that some people create composite indicators for fun – like ferroequinology (trainspotting). It is not, however, everyone's idea of a good way to spend the day. Trainspotting has its hardships; so too, does making MPIs. Uppermost in the minds of the creators of measures like the MPI must be the goal of making indices that are capable of providing policy relevant information (phrases such as 'guide policy'; 'inform policy' pepper the Alkire and Santos 2010a paper). Indeed, there would seem to be little point in making the huge effort involved if MPIs did not have this characteristic.

Policy relevance is not easy to define. If, however, we follow a lead offered by the OPHI website, and accept the word 'useful' as a synonym for it, we obtain some idea of what Alkire *et al* may have in mind. The website positively glows when it comes to explaining why the approach is useful, despite the recognition and acknowledgement of the limitations of the MPI as it currently stands. Here is what it has to say:

"The Alkire Foster method is a single societal poverty measure, but it can be broken down and analysed in a powerful way to inform policy. It can be used to:

- **Break down by population group**. the measure can be broken down (decomposed) by geographic area, ethnicity, or other groups, to show the composition of poverty within and among the groups.
- **Break down by dimension/indicator**. the measure can be broken down (decomposed) after identification to show which deprivations are driving poverty among and within groups.
- **Compare across time**. the measure can be used to monitor changes in poverty and the composition of poverty over time using time series or panel data. The Alkire Foster method reflects other dimensions directly and changes immediately as these change. This makes it an effective monitoring tool because improvements in the dimensions measured, such as health and education, are reflected quickly.
- **Target the poorest groups and beneficiaries of conditional cash transfers, district interventions or public programmes**. The targeting tool can be broken down to show the indicators in which they are most deprived.

- • **Complement other metrics**. The Alkire Foster Method can complement other measures, such as income poverty." [13]

It is clear that no effort has been spared in the quest to ensure that the MPI is technically as rigorous as can be, fitted as it is with the bells and whistles required to ensure that it is consistent with a set of axioms of the sort inspired by those applied to uni-dimensional measures, suitably modified and expanded to accommodate the challenges posed by a multi-dimensional measure (Alkire and Foster, 2009, pp.17ff). The latter quality or attribute; its much vaunted property of decomposability along FGT lines, and its alleged empirical robustness (Alkire and Santos, 2010a, p.65), furnish its creators with the platform on which to announce its virtues, in particular, its policy relevance.

Even if data from high-quality surveys conducted at frequent intervals were available, it is by no means obvious that MPIs could deliver all that is promised. [14] The authors are not so immodest as not to acknowledge that the work of constructing MPIs is seriously impeded by data constraints (implicit in this acknowledgement is the recognition that the resulting measures may not be very good). Nor do they imagine that MPIs are everywhere applicable. [15] This notwithstanding I still find myself wishing that a little more modesty were on display. To talk, for example, of the MPI being "an effective monitoring tool because improvements in the dimensions measured, such as health and education, are reflected quickly"[16] when all that may be available is a single, small, dated survey for a particular country, is more than a little disingenuous. If only the blurb were sufficiently self-confident to announce that the MPI is not a panacea – that there will be times when it will not be useful.

Reflecting on the alleged capabilities of the MPI, it is clear that in order to discharge duties that differ so greatly in scope, the index must take quite distinct forms. The first of these is a set of highly aggregated (i.e., national level) estimates of multi-dimensional poverty, that have been squashed into an international league table.

---

[13] Downloaded from http://www.ophi.og.urk/research/multidimensional-poverty/alkire-foster-method/ 25 October 2011.

[14] The 2010 HDR (and the Alkire and Santos 2010a paper from which the MPIs are drawn) would have been more credible had the authors taken the trouble to indicate which of the estimates possessed the qualities required to deliver the promised results. The same is true for the 2011 HDR.

[15] After estimating MPIs in Europe, Eastern Europe and the Commonwealth of Independent States, Alkire and Santos conclude that they: "… do not believe that the MPI will be able to guide policy significantly in these countries; a different measure is required." (2010a, p.48)

[16] Alkire and Santos concede that "… ordinal variables impede our ability to evaluate the depth of poverty using MPI… " (2010a, p.65)

The estimates are drawn from relatively small international surveys, such as the Demographic and Health Survey (DHS) or World Health Survey (WHS), chosen (reluctantly) by Alkire *et al* to permit comparability (or reduce incomparability).[17]

If the claimed use of the MPI for 'targeting the poorest groups and beneficiaries of conditional cash transfers, district interventions or public programmes' is to be taken seriously, then the other form that the MPI must take is that of comprehensive national (or regional) measure based on some form or other of census. This, it will be argued below, is a tall order.

There is also an 'intermediate' possibility, namely, the estimation of MPIs using surveys other than the DHS and WHS, where available, as has been done in South Africa with the National Income Dynamics Survey (NIDS). The problem they face when doing so, is that of finding appropriate indicators for health and education, for, as will be argued below, their use of the NIDS has not solved the fundamental problem that these two 'dimensions' or 'domains' pose for the construction of a plausible MPI. The resulting estimates would not be suitable for 'targeting the poorest groups' and may not have enough in common with surveys from other countries to allow for the construction of an international league table. Choosing bigger surveys, like the 30 000-household General Household Survey (GHS), conducted annually in South Africa (assuming health and education could be sorted out satisfactorily) does not pay all that much of a dividend – sub-national estimates of many variables cease being useful below the provincial level (2-6 or 7 million people). So, although Alkire's and Foster's warning about mistaking the particular for the general (2011, p.19) needs to be borne in mind, it cannot be taken for granted that 'other specifications' will always be able to make estimation of an MPI possible.

One of the proclaimed uses of the MPI is as an instrument for targeting "… the poorest groups and beneficiaries of conditional cash transfers, district interventions or public programmes". It seems unlikely that this will happen in many places in the near future. A possible basis for the claim lies in the work that Alkire and Seth (2008/2009) performed on a census designed to identify the rural poor in India. Conducted every five years until 1992 among rural households, the census forms the basis of a social assistance programme reaching into every household deemed to fall below the poverty line. A number of aspects of the census have been controversial

---

[17] The bulk of the present work is devoted to an examination of how badly this strategy backfired in South Africa's case, a task rendered easy by the fact that switching to a better survey revealed a substantial increase in the number of multi-dimensionally poor, an increase that cannot be explained by events in South Africa.

over the years – frequent changes have had to be made to deal with these. The abstract of the Alkire and Seth paper informs us that:

> "This paper focuses on the methodology by which India's 2002 Below the Poverty Line (BPL) census data identify the poor and construct a BPL headcount. Using the BPL 2002 methodology and NFHS (National Family Health Survey) data, it identifies which rural families would have been considered BPL were NFHS (National Family Health Survey) data used. It compares these to poor families that would be identified using the same variables with the Alkire Foster multidimensional poverty methodology. It finds that up to 12 per cent of the poor sample population and 33 per cent of the extreme poor could be misclassified as non-poor by the pseudo-BPL method." (2008/2009, p.1)

If the MPIs estimated for the different states are correct, the errors disclosed[18] would be evidence of spectacular injustice. The Alkire and Seth paper has the sub-title: 'A New Proposal'. It does not look as though that proposal has been taken up. Although the Indian government estimates of levels of exclusion and inclusion errors differ, they are equally spectacular. Dissatisfaction with the results of the 2002 BPL census led the Ministry of Rural Development (MRD) to appoint an Expert Group led by Dr Saxena, to 'recommend a more suitable method for conducting the next BPL' (MRD, 2009, p.2).[19]

The report is fascinating, describing procedures utterly remote from those in much developed countries. Based on certain criteria, a sorting process performs an initial separation of the rural population into automatically excluded; automatically included, and possible beneficiaries, subject to score on a multi-dimensional set of criteria. The details do not concern us here – what is important is that after all rural households have been assessed, lists ranking the determinations are publicly displayed. People have the right to object (MRD, 2009, pp.31ff).[20] The total number of BPL households is regulated by estimates of the poverty headcount ratio. The Saxena group, commenting on the existing poverty cut-off rate of 28.3 per cent (MRD, 2009, p.9), noted that cost-of-living increases were such that the cut-off should be raised to at least 50 per cent (a daily calorie intake of 2100), and preferably to 80 per cent (2400 calories daily). The Ministry of Rural Development

---

[18] Alkire and Seth vary poverty cut-offs to test for sensitivity – see pp.29ff

[19] What is probably the 2008 version of the Alkire and Seth paper is referred to in a footnote on p.32 of the Saxena report. The paper is not included among the references on p.37 of the report.

[20] As may be imagined, the problem of benefit capture by elites or middle-class households is serious, as is the arbitrary exercise of power in denying appeals from the poor. Interesting though this is, we have not the time to engage with it.

was not charmed by this suggestion, pointing out in their response to the group's report that it was the job of the Planning Commission to estimate poverty levels for the country (MRD, 2009, p.57). The Planning Commission (in the form of Tendulkar Committee) duly did so, leaving the urban poverty rate at 27.5 per cent, and raising the rural poverty rate to 41.8 per cent (PC, 2009; PC, 2011, p.3).

For someone unfamiliar with the Indian literature, a first encounter with it is thrilling. Sadly, our business here does not permit much more indulgence[21] – rather, it is necessary to extract one vital lesson from the procedure (roughly) described above. The question being addressed is that of the possibility of constructing MPIs that could be used to target the poorest groups and beneficiaries. If that means identifying individual households, then the Indian approach, if it can be made to operate more satisfactorily than it has in the past, would allow government to do so.

With its hint of community-based targeting, the BPL census is not the same as a conventional population census. Something like it, however, is necessary for identifying 'deserving' households.[22] Public display may be avoided, but officials at all levels would have to have access to all of the relevant census data. Participation in conventional population censuses usually has to be encouraged using a carrot and stick approach. The carrot is confidentiality. This places detailed census results completely out of reach of any welfare officer. If a reformer were bent on individual MPI measurement for targeting purposes, a different way of identifying them (which is unlikely to be cheap) is going to have to be found. Without digging too deeply into the matter, it would seem as though the Indian system is unique, and if not unique, then at least quite rare.

If by some miracle, census data were made available, some variant of the Indian approach to analysis (blocks of data released to civil servants at local government

---

[21] A quick trawl through the newspapers disclosed a lively debate. Here is a selection of the articles examined: Smita Gupta, "Centre plans to dovetail caste census with BPL survey", *The Hindu*, New Delhi, May 18, 2011; Rishi Shah, "Economic census delayed again due to lack of personnel", *The Economic Times*, Feb 18, 2012; Rishi Shah, "BPL & caste census first, economic census in 2012", *The Economic Times*, Feb 7, 2011; Sreelatha Menon. "BPL census to assess poverty better: Plan panel", *Business Standard*, New Delhi, Oct 07, 2011; K. Balchand. "No direct inclusion for SC, ST in BPL list", *The Hindu*, New Delhi, April 10, 2011; Special Correspondent. "Munda raps Plan panel poverty index", *The Telegraph*, Calcutta, Sept. 26, 2011.

[22] Population censuses have an unfortunate habit of undercounting the population. South Africa has been particularly bad in this regard – the estimated undercount for the 2001 census was "an alarming 17%". The undercount in Mozambique in 1997 was over five per cent, and in the 2002 Tanzania census it was seven per cent. Other African countries seem not to have done as badly. See Stats SA, 2010, p.8.

level) would probably have to be devised – even in countries with modest populations (say, 10-40 millions), estimating national level indices as the sum of all individual records would be a formidable computing task, one probably best carried on a sample of records.

Any questions?

Policymakers are likely to (should?) demand that information prepared for policy purposes be reasonably 'accurate', especially if there are budgetary implications. One rather obvious measure of 'accuracy' is the confidence interval of the estimate of the value of the index in question – ideally, this should be both known and narrow. An index whose chief known property is that it must be treated as the lower bound of an unknown estimate, whose upper bound is wholly unknown (and unknowable), could conceivably be useful in some circumstances – attempting to make use of it to address poverty, however, is on a par with trying to clap with one hand.

Alkire and Santos (2010a, p.65) are at pains to stress the empirical robustness of the MPI. That property is almost certainly necessary if the index is to be policy relevant. It can be argued that in order for an indicator to be considered empirically robust, the information it gives to policymakers should, at a very minimum, be as precise and as reliable as possible, and as appropriate (not everything needs to be measured to three decimal places!). In addition to this, the index must, as noted above, 'isolate reality with the maximum of clarity'.

The manner in which Alkire and Santos carried out the robustness tests was not adequate – the tests should have been capable of revealing the fragility of South Africa's 2003 MPI. Such tests do not consist solely in playing games with statistics – they begin with a simple question – in view of what we know about the country in question, do these results make sense?

Years of immersion in South African reality alerted me immediately to the fact (now-established)[23] that the 2003 MPI made no sense at all. Suppose, however, that Alkire and Santos had discovered the errors in the 2003 MPI earlier, and had managed to withdraw it before it became public. Had I seen only the 2008 MPI, I am not sure how I would have responded to it – I suspect (but I am not sure) that I might have been sufficiently irritated to have taken the bait because of an energetic

---

[23] It is a relief to record, as Table 1 above does, without having to call upon the wisdom of hindsight, that the Alkire and Santos 'lower bound' estimate of the 2003 MPI was spectacularly incorrect, a 'fact' confirmed by the large changes that Alkire *et al* had to make when they switched from the WHS to NIDS.

dislike of research that makes use of the $1.25/day poverty line, a starvation line that detects roughly half the number of poor that South Africa's food poverty line does (or did). What this suggests is that relying on the intuitions of social scientists is fine when there are gross errors to be detected. It is possible that smaller, but still significant errors could slip through.

Where does all of this leave us? As far as I am aware, none of my colleagues in the poverty and social policy business in South Africa has started digging into the MPI yet. Discussions with some of them revealed a flicker of interest, but no more than that, possibly because there is other, more important work to be done. Of course, this could change rapidly, and may already have done so. It would be comforting to have support for the answer to the question I pose here: Has any other survey been conducted in South Africa that would enable Alkire *et al* to deliver on their promise of an index that can 'guide or inform policy'.

Although the 2008 MPI (HDR 2011) finds more people suffering multi-dimensional poverty than its 2003 counterpart (as we have seen above in Table 1), it is, in my view, still not capable of isolating the reality of the crises in health and education, and their effects on poor people, satisfactorily. Consideration of some of the possible candidates – the General Household Survey (GHS); the Community Survey (CS) – does not offer much hope that an 'off-the-shelf' instrument will serve to improve the MPI to a point where it is capable of making significant contributions to policy formation and/or implementation in South Africa.

In Versions 1 and 2 of the paper, I argued that there was little reason to suspect that Alkire and her co-workers had misinterpreted the survey data from which they drew their conclusions. That being so, apart from the brief encounter above with a few of the somewhat odd figures resulting from Alkire's and Santos' use of the 2003 World Health Survey for South Africa, the paper steered clear of direct confrontation with the MPI estimates *per se*. Rather than engage in pointless checking and recalculation of the MPI from the original data source, the earlier versions of the paper argued that the survey used to generate the South African results (the 2003 WHS) was not able to bear the burden imposed upon it. The limited choice of indicators it allowed bore a major part of the responsibility for estimates so poor that the figures offered no clue as to the extent of multiple deprivation in the country. Instead of casting around for better indicators when the move to the 2008 NIDS data was made, Alkire and her co-workers appear to have stuck with the tried, tested and failed. It is possible that better use could be made of the NIDS data – I have not looked into what the survey offers.

If NIDS does not allow for a more precise analysis of education and health, then it is back to the drawing board for the MPI. The starting point is probably with qualitative research in South Africa. There exists a wealth of analysis of deprivation and its causes, information which, in an ideal world, would guide government policy. As ever, some of the 'facts' give rise to competing explanations of social ills, and hence, of appropriate measures for addressing them. That government does not always (or even often?) act as the evidence suggests it should, bears testimony not only to the ignorance of many policymakers (seemingly a widely-distributed trait), but also and more importantly, to the complexities of policy formation under conditions of uncertainty, usually in the face of pressure exerted by vested interests.

Certain it is though that conditions in the health and education sectors in South Africa were and still are dire, much worse than the trivial numbers produced by Alkire *et al* for the 2003 MPI, and the slightly less trivial numbers thrown up by their MPI for the year 2008, would suggest. To illustrate this, readers are offered an overview of some recent research in these two areas in South Africa. Although there are gaps, the evidence bases are large. They demonstrate, as one would expect, that South Africa is no exception when it comes to the likelihood of the poor suffering most when public services in a country are poor. Before presenting a few morsels from the huge body of information on poverty and its relationship to health and education in South Africa, we need to say a bit about the MPIs themselves.

Section 2 Getting to grips with the MPI

Birthplace of the MPI is the Oxford Poverty & Human Development Initiative (OPHI), located in the Department of International Development in the University of Oxford.[24] Its director is Sabina Alkire. In the short while it has existed, OPHI has been very productive–between 2007 and October 2011, the unit published 45 working papers, several of which have subsequently appeared as journal articles. According to the homepage of the OPHI website, the stated purpose of the initiative is:

> "To build a multidimensional economic framework for reducing poverty grounded in people's experiences and values"

OPHI's most significant intellectual output to date is the Alkire Foster MPI. Obviously, apart from being rigorous (complying with the relevant axioms), an index of such ambition needs, as well, to rest on a coherent theoretical base. In the present paper, we are concerned not so much with whether or not the MPI does the latter (that topic is addressed briefly below), rather, the prime intention is to show that be its foundation never so fine, under certain conditions it can produce garbage, the South African MPI being a case in point. What is offered in this section of the paper is (i) a presentation of the main features of the MPI; (ii) some indication of why its creators regard the MPI as useful; (iii) an indication of why critics of multi-dimensional indices do not; (iv) a glance at the Alkire and Santos story about mismatches between MPIs and income poverty estimates, and (v) finally, a query as to why the work of another Oxford University grouping who produce an index of multiple deprivation (IMD) is ignored by Alkire and her co-workers.

The HDI, the HPI and now the MPI

In 2010, the United Nations Development Programme (UNDP) changed the way that poverty estimates are presented in the annual *Human Development Report* (HDR). The new measure, the Multi-Dimensional Poverty Index (MPI) is constructed by what is referred to in Alkire and Santos (2010a, p.9) as "the Alkire Foster methodology". The authors of the HDR claim that: "The MPI, simple and

---

[24] OPHI papers contain the following acknowledgement: "OPHI gratefully acknowledges support for its research and activities from the Government of Canada through the International Development Research Centre (IDRC) and the Canadian International Development Agency (CIDA), the Australian Agency for International Development (AusAID), and the United Kingdom Department for International Development (DFID) as well as private benefactors.

policy relevant, complements monetary-based methods by taking a broader approach." (UNDP, 2010, p.94)

The MPI[25] takes the place of the Human Poverty Index (HPI), introduced in 1997. According to the HDR, the HPI was "[p]ioneering in its day". Making use, as it did, of: "… country averages to reflect aggregate deprivations in health, education and standard of living… ", one of its limitations was that it: "... could not identify specific individuals, households or larger groups of people as jointly deprived." (UNDP, 2010, p.94)

The MPI, also concerned to assess deprivations in the dimensions (or domains or spheres) of health, education and standard of living, is claimed to address this shortcoming by:

"…capturing how many people experience overlapping deprivations and how many deprivations they face on average." (UNDP, 2010, p.94)

Whether or not the Human Poverty Index (HPI) for South Africa was ever 'policy relevant' is moot – I do not recall coming across any reference to it other than in the HDRs for South Africa, where, presumably, it became inaudible among the general cacophony about poverty (on which, a little more below). That is not at issue here – rather, since the compilers of the MPI have not seen fit to exclude South Africa from their blanket claim about policy relevance, a primary concern in the present paper is to discover if there are grounds for making such an assertion in that country's case.[26]

'Policy relevance' is an elastic concept, as the history of the Human Development Index (HDI), another measure in the HDR stable seeking to combine those three dimensions into an index of development, clearly shows. The HDI, in whose creation, Sen played a part, is first cousin of the MPI. In the 1999 HDR, there is a tribute by Sen to "Mahbub ul Haq, the originator of the Human Development Report". In it, Sen talks of his own:

"…considerable scepticism about trying to focus on a crude index of this kind [the HDI], attempting to catch in one simple number a complex reality about human development and deprivation… "

---

[25] No pretence at adequacy of treatment of the MPI is made here – for those interested in finding out more about MPIs, the relevant papers are no more than a few mouse clicks away, as, indeed, are the 2010 and 2011 *Human Development Reports.*

[26] To be fair to Alkire *et al*, the 2010 HDR does offer a list of limitations of the MPI (see UNDP, 2010, pp.99-100). None of these however, warns users that the policy relevance of any particular MPI may be severely impaired by the limitations in question.

Uppermost in ul Haq's mind, however, was the need to supplant "GNP (an overused and oversold index ...)" as a measure of development. Ultimately, Sen was persuaded by the argument that:

"We need a measure of the same level of vulgarity as GNP—just one number— but a measure that is not as blind to social aspects of human lives as GNP is."

Recognising that ul Huq's intention was to "broaden public interest in the other variables that are plentifully analysed" in the HDR, Sen concedes that "Mahbub got this exactly right", pulling readers into "the large class of systematic tables and detailed critical analyses" using the "attracting power of the HDI" (HDR, 1999, p.23).

One example of the HDI's 'attracting power' in operation in South Africa was the angry contempt aroused in government circles, when it was reported that the country had slipped in the international ranking from position 85 in 1990 (HDR, 1993, p.14) to 120 in 2003 (HDR, 2005, p.225), thus opening the way for reactionary critics to claim that conditions were worse than they had been under apartheid.[27] The incident is worth looking at closely for what it reveals about international league tables.

South Africa's slide down the league table, as anyone who is interested can discover in a matter of minutes if they know where to look, resulted from rapidly falling life expectancy at birth, caused in turn, by the HIV/AIDS epidemic. The exact extent of the fall is a matter of dispute. Although estimates made by those most concerned with demographic statistics differ – the main actors are Statistics South Africa, (Stats SA the official statistics producer), and the Actuarial Society of South Africa (ASSA) builders of the most important non-official demographic model – there is

---

[27] One response was a commission I received from the South Africa's Statistician-General, presumably under instruction from someone high up in government, to probe the HDI for weaknesses. Some were found, but they did not significantly alter the HDI rank (Meth, 2007b). A copy of the paper, which is unpublished, was sent to the UNDP. It was supposed to have been tabled at a UN meeting. Anyone interested may have a copy on application to chasmeth@gmail.com. South Africa's fall in the HDI league table was slow and steady. The media chose to make a huge fuss when the 2005 HDR was published (see Meth, 2007b, pp.4ff), possibly because the HDI trend table it presented enabled users to take a longish view of the way things had changed under ANC rule. In the apartheid era from 1975-1990, the HDI climbed steadily from 0.655 to 0.735. In 1995 it stood at 0.742, slipping to 0.696 in 2000 and 0.658 in 2003. See HDR 2005, p.225. Note that the values in HDI trend tables are revised from time to time, presumably as 'better' data become available. In the 2011 HDR, the HDI reportedly fell from 0.616 in 2000 to 0.599 in 2005, then up to 0.619 in 201. It was ranked in that year at position 123 (p.133).

agreement, at least, that between 2001 and 2005, it fell. For what it is worth, the latest Stats SA figures inform us that in 2001, life expectancy at birth among males was 52.1 years. By 2005, this had dropped to 49.6 years. Corresponding values for females were 57.8 and 53.8 years. The combined effect of these falls was to lower the totals from 55.1 years in 2001, to 51.8 in 2005 (Statistical release P0302, 27 July 2011, p.6).[28]

As far as our story is concerned, the significance of the events described above is twofold: in the first place, as far as I am aware, other than to give rise to irritation in government circles, the behaviour of the HDI does not appear to have had any impact on policy – the battle between AIDS activists and South Africa's Presidency (sheltering behind a curtain of denialism, on which, more below) drew on the vast pile of research conducted in the country. In the second, using the criterion of 'ability to isolate reality adequately', the HDI shows its superiority over the MPI by charting the dramatic fall in the state of 'development' in South Africa, a fall readily traced to the aforementioned falling life expectancy. The significance of this set of circumstances for the choice of indicators for measuring the health dimension in the MPI will become apparent below.

Returning to the story of the 'vulgar' HDI, we discover that at some point after its introduction, it apparently underwent a transformation from ugly duckling, into a resource allocation tool[29] that reportedly reached as far down the chain of jurisdictions as municipalities. Provincial level HDIs are commonplace, because many countries produce Gross Geographic Product (GGP) statistics – estimates of the per capita GGP component can be plugged straight into the HDI calculation.[30] Although many cities are large enough to be treated in the same way (although not

---

[28] The figures given here differ from those used by the UNDP to construct the HDIs. For the year 1999, life expectancy at birth in South Africa was given as 53.9 years (HDR 2001, p.142). The 2002 HDR tells us that life expectancy at birth in South Africa in the year 2000 was 52.1 years (p.151). The corresponding value for the year 2001 in the 2003 HDR was 50.9 years (p.239). The 2007/2008 HDR gives a life expectancy in the year 2005 of 50.8 years (p.231).

[29] Some of these applications were recounted at a UNDP technical workshop in Nairobi in 2007 (Kurukulasuriya, 2007).

[30] The provincial HDIs in the *South Africa Human Development Report 2003* (UNDP, 2003) do this. How reliable they are is an open question. The 2003 SA HDR uses gross geographic product (GGP) data purchased from Quantec, a private provider of national statistics. The firm purchases official statistics, repackages them, making some attempt to render them consistent, then retails them, mainly, apparently, to corporate clients. In some quarters, Statistics South Africa's GGP estimates were said to be a little erratic. A glance at both old (2003) and new (2011) estimates does not disclose anything obviously silly. See, for example, Statistical release P0441, 25 November 2003 and 29 November 2011.

without raising awkward questions), similar estimates for smaller jurisdictions are not generally available. As a result, contemplation of the production of small-area HDIs saw inquiries being made within the UNDP as to what could be used as a substitute. A short, but revealing document giving responses from around the world to a query from the UNDP in Bulgaria on what to use in place of GDP, demonstrated both the difficulty faced by those attempting to find suitable measures to use for small 'economies' that are much more 'open' than any national economy (one of the awkward questions referred to above), as well as the resourcefulness of those proposing solutions to this problem (Bjorkman, 2000).

Looking back on this short history, a few things are apparent. One of them is that the HDI proved its worth in South Africa with its ability to detect the crisis caused by the HIV/AIDS epidemic (something that the MPI in the form used to generate the HDR league tables cannot do). A possibility that must be considered, however, is that Mahbub ul Haq's wishes notwithstanding, the HDI may not attract much attention at all, other than the sort described above. On the clearly negative side, pressing the HDI into uses for which it really was not suited, smacks of desperation – whatever its other failings, the MPI, at least in principle, should be able to make a better contribution to a resource allocation task than the HDI, something that its creators would almost certainly not want to deny. Let us, therefore, delay no longer, our meeting with this reportedly empirically robust, axiom-compliant decomposable creation.

The bare bones of the MPI (and a bit more background)

Tracing a theoretical framework in the MPI is no easy matter (the framework allegedly resides in Sen's 'capability' land). The inspiration for the MPI in the work of Amartya Sen, an intellectual debt frequently acknowledged, is obvious. The section of the HDR devoted to poverty, drawing directly on the work of Alkire and her co-workers states simply that "… [t]he MPI is grounded in the capability approach…"[31] Paying homage to Sen's work in creating the underpinnings of "… the concept and measures of human development… " they find (part of)[32] the imperative (and the challenge) to build a credible multi-dimensional poverty measure in a statement by that worthy which reads as follows:

---

[31] Footnote No. 22 in UNDP, 2010 (p.94) refers to the work of Alkire and Foster 2009; Alkire and Santos 2010; Bourguignon and Chakravarty 2003; Brandolini and D'Alessio 2009.
[32] The introduction to the 2009 Alkire and Foster paper contains a brief history listing other major influences and contributors to the multi-dimensional poverty index debate.

"Human lives are battered and diminished in all kinds of different ways, and the first task... is to acknowledge that deprivations of very different kinds have to be accommodated within a general overarching framework." (Sen, cited in Alkire and Santos, 2010a, p.6)

Noting that "... Sen's perspective has implications for poverty measurement... ", they cite a 1997 paper by Anand and Sen to the effect that:

"The need for a multidimensional view of poverty and deprivation guides the search for an adequate indicator of human poverty." (Alkire and Santos, 2010a, p.6)

Marry this to Sen's capabilities framework, and the intellectual warrant for the pursuit of that will-o-the-wisp, a mashup index[33] to measure multi-dimensional poverty, is signed.

In choosing as major dimensions of the MPI, health, education and standard of living,[34] Alkire *et al* endorse (willingly or unwillingly) a time-honoured custom, one that has seen these three render long service as the most important dimensions of welfare. In the MPI, they are accorded equal weight. Health and education status within any household is measured by two indicators, each of which is weighted equally at 1/6 of the total value of the index. For health, the indicators are:

- "Child mortality – If any child has died in the family
- Nutrition – If any adult or child in the family is malnourished"

For education, they settle upon:

- "Years of Schooling – If no household member has completed 5 years schooling
- Child school attendance – If any school-aged child is out of school in years 1-8"

To gauge the standard of living in any household, they employ six indicators, each weighted at 1/18 of the total value of the MPI. The indicators are:

- "Electricity – If a household does not have electricity

---

[33] The concept is used by Ravallion (2010) who "borrows it from web jargon" (p.3).
[34] Wellbeing or welfare, as the last of the trio is sometimes referred to, is not quite the same as standard of living, often being considered as part of the social wage, itself, a much contested concept. See Meth, 2008.

- Drinking water – If water does not meet MDG definitions or is more than 30 minutes (*sic*) walk away
- Sanitation – If sanitation does not meet MDG definitions, or the toilet is shared
- Flooring – If the floor is dirt, sand or dung
- Cooking Fuel – If they cook with wood, charcoal or dung
- Assets – If the household does not own more than one of: TV, radio, telephone, motorbike or refrigerator, and does not own a car or truck" (Alkire and Santos, 2010a, p.17)

Data constraints oblige Alkire *et al* to treat all members of households as being deprived in any of the ten conditions presented above when one of them is so deprived (Alkire and Santos, 2010a, pp.13ff). When a household suffers a sufficient number of deprivations, the household and all persons in it are deemed to be multi-dimensionally poor.[35] To achieve this status, Alkire and Santos stipulate that the sum of the weighted indicators in which the individuals in that household are deprived should be equal to or greater than 30 per cent of the total value of the index (2010a, p.19). So, for example, individuals in a household whose only asset among those listed above is a radio, in which wood is used for cooking and in which there is no electricity, and which has one child of about eight years of age out of school, would be multi-dimensionally poor.[36]

---

[35] Intra-household inequalities are ignored, a drawback to which the reader's attention is drawn in the discussion of the limitations of the MPI in the HDR (UNDP, 2010, p.100). Not only that, although it is widely acknowledged that defining households adequately is extremely difficult, the possibility that the surveys used by Alkire *et al* may be deeply flawed because of this will be ignored. For a discussion of some of the problems with the concept of 'household', see Randall *et al*, 2011.

[36] To slide into the anecdotal for a moment, when my parent's marriage broke up, my four siblings (all younger) and I, were packed off to live with our grandmother, a widow, in a small village in what was then called East Pondoland (I was eight years old at the time, i.e., I had had two years of education). Granny had spent four years at school (she was, however, both functionally literate and numerate – the three Rs were taken seriously at the end of the 19th century). The house's outside latrine (a long drop) did not comply with MDG guidelines (nor did the slops bucket); the floor in a large part of the house was flagstones grouted with mud and dung (cow dung slurry made a fine floor polish); cooking fuel was wood; baths (infrequent) were in a zinc tub; there was no heating (winters were cold); the village, and thus the house, had no electricity, so there was no radio (TV was not introduced into South Africa until 1975); lighting was provided by candles and paraffin lanterns; there was no telephone (the nearest was ¾ mile away at the Post Office); there were neither motor-bike nor refrigerator, and certainly no car, truck or bicycle – the only 'vehicle' was a wheelbarrow. Breakfast was invariably *mielie pap* (ground maize porridge) occasionally with home-made butter, evening meals were often *imifino* (a wild leafy

Conspicuous by its absence from the MPI is employment (the bringer of income), the lack of which constitutes a more serious deprivation than several of those listed above. Not being able to exercise the capability of engaging in the activity widely regarded as the mark of non-dependence, leads to an all-too-familiar catalogue of social and personal misery – anyone doubting this need only refer to the portrait of the Rainbow Nation with which this study commenced. Any misgivings about its accuracy will rapidly be dispelled by a little digging into the substantial literature on which the sad picture it offers, is based. The Alkire and Santos position on the matter of employment is that:

"We have stated that developing countries in higher stages of development would need a variant of the MPI, with different indicators and/or cutoffs to reveal the type of deprivations experienced there. Including indicators on employment, quality of education, empowerment, and using higher cutoffs for the living standard variables are possibilities for such a variant version. This is not to say that these other dimensions are not important in the less developed countries (there, it is a matter of missing data). Nor is it the case that we should change the cutoffs for the least developed countries. The MPI is an index of acute poverty, and that is what it reflects. Its possible variant would reflect a different type of poverty and would be relevant in medium and high human development countries." (2010a, p.64)

One makes of this claim what one will – it seems to me that data on employment, unemployment and non-economic activity are likely to be at least as good as, and possibly better than as those on child mortality. The World Bank appears to have information on youth unemployment and NEETs (young people not in employment, education or training) for sub-Saharan, Latin American and Caribbean countries (Freije, 2012). Some of the countries in these regions are precisely those from which one would least have expected data to be available. It would be interesting to know what the sources are of their figures, and to know how reliable they are. In any event, among the tentative conclusions reached by the Bank is that while open youth unemployment is not closely associated with poverty, the:

---

vegetable) and *umngqusho* (samp and beans), but we were not malnourished. An important 'luxury', it being South Africa in the 1940s, was the services of an even poorer domestic worker. The score for the household using the Alkire and Santos weights would have been about 7 or 8/18 (39-44 per cent). The world is mightily changed since then, but someone living today as we did then could not reasonably be described as acutely poor – poor, yes, but multi-dimensionally deprived – certainly not.

"NEET rate in the developing world are mostly explained by low school attendance and strongly associated to (*sic*) low levels of income" (Freije, 2012, p.14)

How many individuals and households, one wonders, suffer acute poverty (partly) because young people cannot afford to go to school, cannot find work, and do not have the resources to gain access to training, always supposing that at the end of it, there would be jobs for them to do? To jump ahead in our story, it is the Alkire *et al* concern to draw up an international league table from a limited number of survey sources that leads to the exclusion of employment from the list of deprivations.

Moving on from what is not in the MPI, back to what it is, we note that an important property of the indices is their decomposability, a property they share with the FGT income/expenditure poverty measures (Foster, Greer and Thorbecke, 1984). Decomposability posits "… that overall poverty is a population share weighted average of subgroup poverty levels." (Alkire and Foster, 2011, p.9).[37] This allows poverty to be studied by any identifiable sub-groups, e.g., region or ethnicity (but not by gender?).

Reflecting on the menu above, one sees that in constructing it, a number of assumptions and judgements have had to be made:

- The number of dimensions had to be specified
- Once that was done, the relative weights of each dimension had to be specified
- Within each dimension, appropriate indicators had to be found
- When found, the number of indicators in each dimension had to be specified
- Each indicator had to have a weight assigned to it

After all of that had been completed, the selection of a cutoff point for separating the poor from the non-poor (the 30 per cent) had to be made. In short, creation of the MPI is an exercise that requires several leaps in the dark. Inevitably, this entails the substitution of the judgement of a suitably-qualified technician (academic) for the revealed will of the people involved. Although Alkire and her co-workers go to great lengths to explain and justify their choices, arbitrariness in many of them is unavoidable. Given this, it does not seem unreasonable to be a little sceptical of their claim to be 'measuring' poverty.

---

[37] The Foster of the FGT measures and the Foster who collaborates with Alkire, are one and the same (I think).

Possibly anticipating criticism, Alkire *et al* cover their backs with statements showing how aware they (undoubtedly) are of the need for popular participation in the construction of the MPI. Apropos the assignment of weights, for example, they quote Sen saying that:

"It is … crucial to ask in any evaluative exercise … how the weights are to be selected. This judgmental exercise can be resolved only through reasoned evaluation. [I]n arriving at an agreed range for social evaluations (e.g., in social studies of poverty), there has to be some kind of a reasoned consensus on weights or at least on a range of weights. This is a social exercise and requires public discussion and a democratic understanding and acceptance… " (Sen, cited in Alkire and Santos, 2010a, p.18).

Attempts at soliciting the views of those whose circumstances are supposed to be represented by the MPI have been made by its compilers. A box in the 2010 HDR (UNDP, 2010, p.95) gives examples of families suffering multiple deprivation. These are drawn from field studies conducted as part of the background research for the MPI. As one of the "mechanisms" relied on for the selection of the 2010 HDR dimensions, Alkire and Santos list first:

"… the literature arising from *participatory exercises*, which engage a representative group of participants as reflective agents in making the value judgments to select focal capabilities." (2010a, p.12, emphasis in original)

In the concluding remarks of their paper, Alkire and Santos comment on the broad clusters of deprivations they have uncovered, and then observe that:

"Each country deserves an analysis that thoroughly scrutinizes the particular clustering of deprivations as well as the geographical, religious, and ethnic distribution of poverty." (2010a, p.64)

To be of any value, 'thorough scrutiny' include 'public discussion and a democratic understanding and acceptance' of as many as possible of the issues listed above as requiring judgement to be exercised. Alkire and Santos claim that they:

"… are fully aware of the limitations of the MPI, and [that they] advocate improving data collection in the developing world to overcome these issues." (2010a, p.64)

Brief reference was made above to the fact that in the face of missing values among critical variables, the MPIs for a number of countries in the 2010 HDR, including South Africa, were to be regarded as 'lower bounds' only. Alkire and Santos did not propose upper limits, presumably because they could not. As was pointed out in Versions 1 and 2 of the paper, the likely explanation for that failure was the faulty manner in which the attempt to 'isolate reality' in difficult-to-measure areas like education and health had been made.

Everyone supports the call for more and better data (except possibly survey respondents). Unless, however, more careful thought is given to the business of (a) finding better indicators for health and education, and (b) finding surveys that can deliver good quality estimates of the magnitudes of the relevant variables, the MPI should continue to be treated with more than just the usual caution.

A hunt for theory in the MPI plus sundry other criticisms

Criticisms of the MPI extend beyond the issue of the extravagance of its claimed relevance. The following issues (not in order of importance) also spring to mind:

- one involves looking at the impetus to produce composite (or, more picturesquely 'mashup') indices, while
- another concerns the validity of the theoretical foundations of the index
- a third, the method by which the index is assembled, and
- a fourth with the pros and cons of using such measures

A few thoughts on each are offered below, commencing with an observation about how reassuring it is to find that others have discovered the claims made on behalf of the MPI to be somewhat overblown. In December 2010, Alkire presented a paper (referred to as Alkire, 2011) at a conference in Paris on 'how well we measure development'. It is clear from the tone of the comments offered by the discussant of the paper that it (the paper) is an attempt of sorts to address some of the criticisms made after the MPI was launched. The final paragraphs of the discussant's observations read as follows:

> "The paper reflects the laudable desire to acknowledge and deal with issues raised in the rather extensive dialogue that took place after the initial release of the MPI, and certainly tones down the claims made in Alkire and Santos (2010a). While honest and generous, it also makes a reader wonder what has been achieved so far!

> They ... confound the key issue of whether a composite measure of multidimensional poverty (such as the MPI) does better than a collection of indicators deployed carefully and intelligently. ...

In my view, while the considerable effort of the author and her team should be applauded, the jury is still out on the matter." (Taffesse, 2011, p.95)[38]

As to the question of the impetus to produce composite indices, it is perhaps useful to point out that not all dabblers in the arcane art of juggling indicators feel comfortable about converting sets of these things into 'actual measures of poverty'. Berthoud *et al*, for example, say that:

"One view is that poverty consists of a lack of resources (one of whose main symptoms is a low standard of living). This view requires only a weak set of assumptions about deprivation scores – they are just an indicator, used to identify groups at risk of poverty or to calibrate a poverty line.

An alternative view is that poverty consists of low living standards (one of whose main causes is lack of resources). This view requires a much stronger set of assumptions about deprivation scores – they have to be comprehensive enough and reliable enough to be treated as an actual measure of poverty.

The analysis in this study is based on the view that no index can support the strong set of assumptions required to treat it as a direct measure of poverty. It uses the weak set of assumptions which treats the survey data as just an indicator." (2004, pp.1-2, emphasis in original)

If we rephrase the 'alternative' view above, substituting 'multiple deprivation' for 'low living standards' and 'want or absence of capabilities' for 'lack of resources', making strong assumptions about deprivation scores would enable us to churn out an MPI. Why would anyone want to do such a thing? What inspires them?

One possible explanation is that like all good scientists, the MPI's creators were alive to the virtues of using Occam's razor to pare away flab, exposing a single information-rich number that can measure poverty in many dimensions. After all, it was James Foster, who with his colleagues Erik Thorbecke and Joel Greer, developed the widely-used FGT $P\alpha$ poverty measures, and, in doing so, brought economy to the measurement of the extent, depth and severity of uni-dimensional poverty.[39] In striving to do something similar for multi-dimensional poverty, he and

---

[38] As far as the 2003 South African MPI is concerned (Alkire and Santos, 2010a) the jury need deliberate no longer – the pair are guilty of dumping rubbish onto the research community, rubbish ineffectually wrapped in a plea for clemency that says 'sorry, but the dataset we were obliged to use can only tell us where the lower limit of your poverty problem may lie – is that of any use to you?' No!
[39] For discussion of some of the problems involved in using FGT ratios to disclose the dimensions of income poverty, see Meth, 2011. Non-compliance of the P_2 measure with the

Alkire are thus not only following a path well-trodden, they are also conforming to one of the standards by which scientific theory is judged (rightly or wrongly). Here it is, as articulated Edward Wilson:[40]

"The elegance, we can fairly say the beauty, of any particular scientific generalisation is measured by its simplicity relative to the number of phenomena it can explain." (1978 [2001], p.10)

The MPI, of course, is not a theory; by itself, it cannot explain anything (presumably, nobody claims that it can), rather, it is analogous to a box, the three dimensions (aptly named) of the MPI mimicking height, breadth and depth, which, when combined in a particular way, yield an index called volume.[41] As is the case with the MPI, the (somewhat arbitrary) conventions agreed upon to measure the dimensions of a box may be varied, if desired, to accentuate certain properties, and, like social reality, boxes also have many other properties or characteristics, some not easily measurable. If we agree, however, that the essence of a box is its capacity to contain other objects,[42] then any object conforming to that specification is a box – its dimensions provide one accurate measure of its capacity to carry out its function. Additional capacities, such as an ability to contain objects successfully it the box is to be moved from place to place are a function of other variables such as the mass of the objects, and the physical properties (other than size) of the box. In principle, ascertaining whether or not a box has these capacities, is straightforward.

The MPI, by contrast, elegant though it undoubtedly is, has no capacity other than the ability to inform us that when two or more estimates of the magnitude (or presence or absence) of certain variables are combined in a particular way, they generate a number. By construction, the number conforms to a set of rules or axioms required to make it behave appropriately when any of its component variables undergo change. Whether or not the number represents a true estimate of the extent and severity of the condition called poverty which some people may be experiencing, cannot be settled without theory being invoked to explain what

---

transfer sensitivity axiom is considered on pp.16-19 of the paper, with a hypothetical, but plausible example showing how both positive P_1 and P_2 results, when given only as ratios, can be overwhelmed by rising inequality (such as that experienced in South Africa).

[40] Wilson's prophetic suggestion that we were about to witness the joining of the two cultures of Western life, the social and the natural sciences through the blending of the former with biology (1978 [2001], p.9), has been triumphantly borne out. See, for example, Bowles and Gintis, 2011.

[41] Playing games in n-dimensional space is difficult.

[42] We could be pedantic and insist that it be a particular shape, e.g., rectangular, and that beyond certain sizes, the name changes. That, however, would not alter the essential nature of a box.

poverty is, and how the indicators chosen to 'measure' it, actually do what they are supposed to. In other words, the search for theoretical validity of the MPI has to be conducted among stories about what poverty is, and how/why it is that the indicators selected to measure poverty are causally connected to poverty.[43]

As is clear from the frequent references in the work of Alkire and her colleagues,[44] the story told about poverty is that developed by Sen over a number of years, and a fine story it is too, for the most part.[45] Capturing the subtlety of that story in an index is, however, more than a little challenging. The formidable obstacle course of assumptions and judgements that must be traversed to select and then turn a package of indicators into a poverty measure without the clear guidance of a theoretical framework appears to hold few terrors for Alkire and her co-workers – they seem to leap blithely over them to join the long list of researchers who have produced what have come to be described as 'mashup' measures (Ravallion, 2010). Unlike 'dashboard' measures, i.e., those that require the user to respond appropriately to a number of separate indicators, mashup measures scramble (or mash together) many indicators to produce a single index. Addressing the problem of theory as it applies to the HDI (and the MPI), Ravallion remarks that:

> "Some mashup indices have alluded to theoretical roots, to help give credibility. However, there is invariably a large gap between the theoretical ideal and what is implemented. For example, the HDI claims support from Sen's writings arguing that human capabilities are the relevant concept for defining welfare or well-being ….. Yet it is quite unclear how one goes from Sen's relatively abstract formulations in terms of functionings and capabilities to the specific mashup index that is the HDI. …. It is clearly a large step indeed from Sen's (often powerful) theoretical insights to the idea of human development found in the HDRs, and an even bigger step to the specific measure that is the HDI.
>
> A similar comment applies to the MPI." (Ravallion, 2010, pp.9-10)

As the 'box' analogy offered above suggested, the movement 'from Sen's relatively abstract formulations in terms of functionings and capabilities to the specific

---

[43] Similar strictures apply, of course, to the single indicator that constitutes a uni-dimensional poverty measure.

[44] A typical example (to add to those already offered) may be found in OPHI working paper No. 32 published a couple of years ago, where it is asserted that the MPI methodology: "…embodies Sen's …. view of poverty as capability deprivation …" (Alkire and Foster, 2009, p.5).

[45] A good (sympathetic) introduction to the capabilities approach and its critics may be found in Clark, 2005. There are frequent references in the paper to work done in South Africa.

mashup index that is the MPI', should begin in discussions about the mechanisms[46] by which the MPI 'dimensions' for the HDR are selected. Many studies have shown that people's perceptions of what it means to be poor extend a good deal further than health, education and the few assets in Alkire's and Santos' 'living standards' dimensions – something to which the authors themselves draw attention (2010a, p.12). For practical purposes such as creating an index that identifies those suffering acute multiple deprivation, the number of dimensions needs to be (?) or is (?) pared down to some irreducible (?) minimum. They inform us that the advice offered by Sen in this matter is that:

"In the context of choosing capabilities that have a moral weight akin to human rights, [he] has suggested focusing on dimensions that are of a) *special importance* to the society or people in question, and b) *social influenceable* (*sic*) – which means that they are an appropriate focus for public policy …." (Alkire and Santos, 2010a, p.12)

Translating that into practice, they report that:

"… the selection of the 2010 HDR dimensions has relied on the following mechanisms:

    a. The first is the literature arising from *participatory exercises*, ….
    b. The second is the use of some *enduring consensus,* ….
    c. The third is *theory based*, as in the many philosophical or psychological accounts of basic needs, universal values, human rights, and so on.
    d. The fourth and the binding constraint is *whether the data exist*." (2010a, p.12, emphasis in original)

As research resources (or constraints), mechanisms *a*, *b*, and *d* are relatively unproblematic – it is in mechanism *c* that the difficulties lie. If selection is 'theory based', then it is necessary to demonstrate that a theory such as the 'capabilities' package can make the transition from a set of abstract concepts (undoubtedly powerful) into something capable of being measured. Yet as the Abstract of a recent OPHI working paper declares:

"More than three decades after Sen's first formulation of the so-called "capability approach", practitioners have yet to measure a capability set. This raises fundamental questions about the empirical viability of Sen's approach." (Silva-Leander, 2011)

---

[46] A couple of these mechanisms have been alluded to above.

Far from being an arch-critic, the writer of the passage cited immediately above, appears to be keen to salvage the conceptual approach – his proposed route is illuminated (dimly?) by Immanuel Kant. There is, however, no mistaking the obstacles that the capabilities measurement project has to surmount, something that Sen recognises, as the following paragraph shows:

> "… several proponents of the capability approach [reportedly among them, Sen himself] have suggested that, for the sake of measurement, practitioners may have to "be content with achievements, instead of capabilities" … However, as Alkire points out, such an approach "would be blind to people's agency … and to their opportunity freedom". Furthermore, it is unclear what value-added a functionings-based interpretation of the capability approach could offer over existing approaches such as the basic needs approach …. This begs the question of knowing whether Sen's capability approach can provide a viable operational alternative to neoclassical welfare economics, or whether it may just be, to paraphrase Atkinson, a powerful theoretical insight without real practical applications …." (Silva-Leander, 2011, p.1)

There is nothing equivocal about his claim that: 'practitioners have yet to measure a capability set'. This is a trifle odd – first of all, it emanates from within the OPHI camp, so presumably, has been viewed by peers. Secondly, the assertion casts doubt on the work of contributors to two branches of the cottage industry devoted to showing that capabilities are indeed measurable. One of these is the Capabilities Measurement Project (CMP), located in the Open University. Its director is Prof Paul Anand, who is also Research Associate in the Health Economics Research Centre in the University of Oxford. In May 2008, Prof Anand gave a presentation with the title "Beyond GNP and Current HDI: An Overview of The Capabilities Measurement Project", at an Oxford University Workshop on Measurement of Freedom. Reviewing the results of various attempts to measure capabilities, Anand declares (encouragingly? defiantly? defensively?) on the second last slide of his PowerPoint presentation that: "It IS possible to measure capabilities…" (emphasis in original).[47] Is it possible that Anand and Silva-Leander have not discussed the question of measurability?

Pursuing similar aims to the CMP is an international grouping of scholars (there is much overlap with the CMP) who are members of the Human Development and Capability Association (HDCA). In essence, the HDCA's mission is to advance scholarship which applies the capabilities approach to development, in the widest possible sense. Past presidents include Sen (the founding president), Martha

---

[47] Downloaded from http://www.open.ac.uk/ikd/projects_capabilitiesmeasurement.shtml, 10 December 2011. There are dozens of papers on the website.

Nussbaum and Frances Stewart. Anthony Atkinson is currently president-elect and Sabina Alkire is vice president – the association's list of fellows is star-studded. The HDCA publishes an E-Bulletin. If one takes a look at issue Number 14 (June 2009),[48] which was dedicated to 'Collecting Capability Data', the first thing one finds is a short piece by Anand, giving a report on progress in the measurement business.

Something about the tone of Anand's approach to the subject matter elicits a more sympathetic response than does Alkire's. Searching for an explanation of the antipathy that her mode of presentation excites in me (and others[49]), I wondered if it was to be found in a comparison of the degree of assertiveness with which they present their findings. In the 2010a Alkire and Santos paper, reasons are given for why a decision was taken (despite major data constraints)[50] to go ahead with the creation and publication of the international league table for the 100-plus countries on the basis of the three dimensions of health, education and standard of living. The reasons (given on pp.12-13) are of no particular interest here – what is important is that Alkire and Santos considered it appropriate to use the available data, warts and all, calling as they did so, for more and better data in the future. Given the difficulties, however, of persuading governments to engage in the expensive activity of conducting large surveys, the data constraints to which they refer are going to persist for years.

Detailed country studies will doubtless become available in time, but until then it would seem sensible not to make too much fuss about how important the capability approach is for measuring multi-dimensional poverty for international comparative purposes. To lapse into the vernacular, all that Alkire and Santos are taking into account at present is the set of bog-standard variables that can be generated by any considered view of the human predicament – as they themselves point out, their selection of the 'dimensions' of health, education and standard of living "is theory based, as in the many philosophical or psychological accounts of basic needs, universal values, human rights, and so on".[51]

---

[48] Downloaded from http://www.capabilityapproach.com/pubs/Maitreyee14_June_09.html on 9April 2012.

[49] Tafesse's remark above about 'toning down the claims' suggests that I am not the only one to respond adversely to the Alkire and Santos (2010a) paper.

[50] They managed to scrape together enough information to do so – as the South African case shows, at least some of it is garbage.

[51] Twenty five years ago, I was teaching public sector economics – when it came to analysing government expenditure and its funding, the standard starting point was with HEW – health, education and welfare (a somewhat broader concept than standard of living) – the emphasis probably came from using Richard and Peggy Musgrave's *Public Finance in Theory and Practice* as prescribed text. These are the things on which governments spend

If their selection of the dimensions of health, education and standard of living, and the set of indicators by which they can be measured were really guided by the capabilities approach, then either the approach itself, or their use of it is too blame for the fact that they could not even detect a major epidemic, a health and education sector in crisis, and large-scale social unrest because of delivery failure on the part of the South African government. Until the league table results have been subject to careful scrutiny, there can be no guarantee that the estimates for other countries given in the annual HDRs,[52] are not infected in the same way that the South African figures are – why, one might ask, the rush to get the index into print?

Apart from the outburst referred to above, those bits of Anand's (and his co-worker's) research at which I have glanced (Anand 2005; Anand *et al* 2005; Anand *et al* 2007; Anand *et al* 2009), seem more considered (and less strident) – a different proposition altogether from the three-dimensioned Alkire international league table stuff, whose claimed link with the capabilities approach looks like being slender for a long while to come.

It is an unusual student of the discipline who did not feel that those parts of conventional economics that travel under the heading 'welfare economics' were not wholly satisfying (*pace* Pigou *et al*). According to Anand (2005, p.300) "some of the main differences between a capability approach and welfare economics are as follows:

- an emphasis on the options people have, as opposed to the activities they undertake
- the variety of material capabilities gives rise to a multivariate approach to wellbeing
- capabilities may make interpersonal comparisons easier than is the case under some ethical approaches—many economists are willing to take for granted that interpersonal comparisons of utility are impossible

---

most of the revenue raised by taxes – in the UK in 2008-2009, for example, identifiable per capita public expenditure on services amounted to £7971. Of that, £3222 went to social protection; £1796 to the National Health Service; £1349 to education, and £841 to transport, public order and safety – i.e., 80 per cent on HEW, 11 per cent on transport, public order and safety and the rest on 'other' (Crawford *et al*, 2009, p.34).

[52] South Africa's 2010 HDR results 'improve' in the 2011 HDR because of the switch to a larger (better) survey. It would be interesting to see how many other countries in their tables would or do enjoy a similar improvement.

- the capabilities approach is driven partly by the inadequacy of preferences (desires) as a measure of a person's interests, in particular, difficulties arising from adaptive preferences"[53]

What the capabilities approach offers is a partial escape from the clutches of utility theory and its problematic maximands. It looks as though some capabilities or capacities may be measurable, but it also looks as though other may not, at least not without a good deal of difficulty. It also looks as though as an approach, capabilities have the edge on utility – possibly because the former is a 'framework capable of being used to generate theories, while the utilitarian approach is a theory'. In some circumstances, they may be able to do the same job, but for the most part, they probably cannot (Anand, 2005, p.303). This and more, one gets from a reading of his work and that of his co-workers. The 'more' looks like this – after a long and detailed analysis of data from the British Household Panel Survey (BHPS) the following caveat is offered:

> "A valid criticism of our findings is that our measures of capabilities may in fact be measures of functionings. This partly results from the circular nature of the relationship. Is health which limits your activities a capability in that it restricts the potential choices you can make, or is it rather a functioning, the result of the choices you made from your capability set to e.g. smoke or drink?" (Anand *et al*, 2005, p.43)

The paper from which that caveat comes considered a wide variety of 'capabilities'. A more focused paper by Anand (2005), looked at a micro-level topic – the right to die – and a macro-level issue – the problems thrown up for resource allocation decisions by the use of the Quality Adjusted Life Years (QUALY) approach in the health sector (sometimes referred to as the 'had a good innings' approach). Crudely, the use of this criterion for maximising the value of health outcomes could be ageist – given two patients of different age, both of whom would die without a certain treatment, and both of whom would survive having had it, treating the younger of the two would probably generate more QUALYs. The capabilities approach cannot solve this ethical problem (it is highly unlikely to yield measures of many

---

[53] The adaptive preferences problem arises from the possibility that: "people might adapt to certain unfavorable circumstances and any self-evaluation in terms of satisfaction or happiness will in this case necessarily be distorted." Evaluation of wellbeing in terms of functionings and capabilities is claimed to offer a "more objective picture of people's life". If adaptation takes place, so runs the argument, subjective views become an unreliable source of information on which to assess wellbeing. This notion has been challenged (Teschl and Comim, 2005, p.229), who argue that: "It becomes clear that adaptation can be a positive as well as a negative phenomenon and that the adaptive preference critique had a particular narrow view on adaptation."

capacities). It does, however, broaden the debate about what health systems should be seeking to achieve, as does the glance at a choice many of us have to face – the right, in, say the face of debilitating or terminal disease, to make informed choices about treatment (Anand, 2005, p.300).

Less dogmatic practitioners than Alkire and her colleagues end up making much more tentative claims about the possibilities of measurement. A recent paper by Lorgelly *et al* (2010), looking at 'Outcome Measurement in Economic Evaluations of Public Health Interventions' using the capabilities approach, said in their conclusion that:

> "To operationalise the approach for use in economic evaluations, it is necessary to generate an index whereby an individual's capability (or capability set) is described by a single composite number. This involves a number of challenges. Key among these is the need to identify a legitimate capability space and then to accurately measure relative preferences for each capability. Indices, and preference measurement more generally, raise the issues of which valuation technique to use, whether and how to anchor the index, and how to control for adaptation."[54] (pp.2283-2284)

A catalogue of obstacles like that should be sufficient to discourage anyone – it probably will not. Worshippers at the capabilities temple, not content with having made the debate about welfare or wellbeing much more interesting, will almost certainly push on regardless, endlessly chanting the 'need more data' mantra.

A recent review of the Alkire Foster methodology arrived at the following conclusion:

> "The current Multidimensional Poverty Index method of Alkire and Foster represents a significant advance. However, the fundamental theoretical problem with the Alkire and Foster modified headcount (H) method (M_0) is that although the mathematics are elegant and it has desirable axiomatic properties, this cannot possibly compensate for a methodology which may not produce valid and reliable deprivation indicators and a dimensional structure which may be highly biased." (Gordon and Nandy, 2012, p.79)

Amen! to that. A dip in the (large) pool of literature filled by the capabilities approach suggests that the journey from Sen's 'relatively abstract formulations'[55] to

---

[54] By this, I assume they refer to the 'adaptive preference' problem.

[55] Some of these abstractions are hotly disputed as the following passage about 'absolute' poverty clearly shows: "Townsend has consistently argued for over 50 years ….. that all

the MPI cannot be made because many capabilities are non-measurable, or if they are measurable, require such complex tests that collecting and collating the necessary evidence becomes too difficult. Even if it proved to be the case that some capabilities could be measured, that would not alter the fact that Alkire and Santos have made a pretty bad job of trying to do so in South Africa. The measurement of achieved outcomes in three spheres – health, education and welfare (a term of several meanings, among them, standard of living) – if it is well done, gives some indication of whether certain basic needs are met (or not, as the case may be). There is obviously some connection between this and capabilities (or the lack of them). Uncovering the extent and nature of those capabilities, it seems to me, is going to require much more qualitative and quantitative research than has already been done – a stripped-down statistical analysis, on which compromises have had to be made because of data constraints will not do.

Enough now of this – suffice it to say at this point, that in the rush to have the MPI installed in a central position in the poverty measurement business, the question raised by Taffesse, namely, that of whether it: "does better than a collection of indicators deployed carefully and intelligently…" remains unanswered.

Let us change direction and travel via a link on the website of the Capabilities Measurement Project (the endeavour glanced at above) to the site for the '2011 New Directions in Welfare Conference' that took place at the OECD in Paris, where a paper by Joumard *et al* (2011) is to be found. The paper, a little treasure trove, treats of composite (or mashup indices) in a couple of places, in the process, introducing readers to the work of one Peter Smith. The piece by Smith of particular interest here appeared in a volume presenting the proceedings of a conference (Smith, 2002) organised by the OECD, held in Ottawa in 2001, a conference whose aim was to reflect on "… how best to report and use performance measures to build more effective health systems." (2002, p.3) Impetus for this conference came partly from the ruckus inspired by the World Health Organization's attempt to "… rank the performance of health systems in individual nations… ", the results of which were published in the *World Health Report 2000*. (Smith, 2002, p.7).

In his contribution, "Developing Composite Indicators for Assessing Health System Efficiency", Smith, after working his way through some of the technical aspects of

conceivable definitions of poverty – even those that purport to be absolute definitions – only have meaning relative to the society in which a person lives. If Townsend is correct, then Sen's claim that poverty is absolute in the "space of the capabilities" is understandable in the same way that the concept of unicorns, fairies and a loving god are understandable. However, there is no more real world meaning to the claim that poverty is absolute in capability space than the claim that poverty is absolute in fairy space." (Gordon, 2008, p.171)

the construction of mashups, casts a glance at the strong and weak points of four attempts to build such things. They were: United States Medicare – seven dimensions, 23 indicators; Canadian health care, six dimensions, 15 indicators; British health authorities, six indicators, and *World Health Report 2000*, five dimensions, some measured by single indicator, others by an index, and others by key informant reports (Smith, 2002, pp.298-304). Of varying quality, the reports can be mined for a list of 'dos' and 'don'ts'. Smith duly does so – the pros and cons of composite measures are given on p.308. These, plus others drawn from a paper by Saisana and Tarantola (2002) make their way in condensed form into the Joumard *et al* (2011) paper. They are reproduced below.

On the plus side:

- "Summarise complex or multidimensional issues in view of supporting decision-making
- Are easier to interpret than many separate indicators
- Facilitate the task of benchmarking countries
- Monitor progress of countries over time on complex issues
- Place issues of country performance and progress at the centre of the policy debate
- Facilitate communication with the general public (*i.e.* citizens, media, etc.) and promote accountability"

On the minus side they listed the following:

- "May disguise serious failings in some dimensions and increase the difficulty of identifying remedial action
- May send misleading policy messages, be misinterpreted or misused, *e.g.* to support a desired policy, if they are poorly constructed or lack transparency
- Invite simplistic policy conclusions and may lead to inappropriate policies if dimensions of performance that are difficult to measure are ignored or poorly represented
- The selection of indicators and weights is not straightforward and could be subject to political pressures
- May make it difficult to account for complementarities across policies" (Joumard *et al*, 2011, p.42)

Most of the conclusions drawn above apply directly to the MPI. On reflection, if I were asked to hazard a guess as to whether MPIs of the type offered in the HDRs could produce a similar response among policy-makers as do health assessments of the type described in Smith (2002), my gut response would be to say no. While all composite measures could lull users into accepting dubious results as plausible guides to courses of action (as Smith has argued, confidence can be misplaced), I suspect that the narrower focus of a health review, and the greater choice of indicators, render it less likely to fail than the MPIs considered in the present paper. In other words, while a carefully constructed MPI, using appropriate indicators and a reliable data base, may be useful, an international league table based on shaky sources and inappropriate indicators, may not.

As far as the MPI is concerned, my guess is that except in countries so lacking in resources as to be unable to perform their own analyses of development, it can, and will be ignored. Countries without the necessary technical expertise could be exposed to at least two of the dangers outlined above, the 'misleading policy messages', and the 'simplistic policy conclusions', if the international experts and consultants whose job it will be to construct measures like the MPI, get it wrong.

Although Smith concludes that:

"… there are strong arguments in principle for seeking to report composite indicators of health system performance… "

note should be taken of his warning that with the:

"… practice of developing indicators [still being] in its infancy… … premature publication will lead to seriously adverse responses from health systems." (2002, p.309)

As Alkire and Santos admit, data constraints, which they hope in future will be eased, place tight limits on what can and cannot be used as indicators for building an international league table. How long it will be before the constraints are relaxed is anybody's guess. In the meantime, it may be useful to separate the MPIs into those in which some reliance can be placed; those like the 2008 South African MPI that are dubious, and those like the 2003 MPI that are rubbish.

It may, however, be the case that while the cleverness that went into creation of the intellectual edifice that is the MPI is much to be admired, it should be with the wonder one would reserve for, say, a Fabergé egg, allied to a feeling that the MPI is about as useful as one. This seditious train of thought was sparked by Anand's comment, reported above, that:

"… capabilities may make interpersonal comparisons easier than is the case under some ethical approaches—many economists are willing to take for granted that interpersonal comparisons of utility are impossible."

While there may not be a firm theoretical basis on which to make interpersonal comparisons, the brute fact of policy implementation in the real world is that such comparisons have to be, and are made every day. Many of the decisions depend on a crass index such as household or personal income – a penny over the limit and you fail to qualify. Social protection systems can, however, be designed to avoid the 'benefit cliff edge' caused by the use of a crude welfare indicator like income.[56] Given the multitude of benefits available in welfare states, it is the case that 'interpersonal comparisons' are made to cover a wide range of deprivations. Although many or most of them are income-based, the fact is that if an individual or household suffers a particular deprivation, or set of deprivations, obtaining relief is not all that difficult. In South Africa, for example, 'passing' a light-touch means test gains access to the Child Support Grant. Obtaining the Older Person's Grant (state old age pension) is also not too difficult. Disability benefits are more rigorously controlled (both the pension and the disability benefit are much higher than median incomes). Households that cannot afford electricity are eligible for free basic minimum provision. The same applies to water, as it does to sanitation Hospital care is free for pregnant women and children under the age of six (albeit of dubious quality)[57] – means-tested charges are levied thereafter. Free housing is supposed to be provided for those earning under R3500 per annum, and subsidised housing for those earning less than R7000 per annum. Schooling is free for the poorest 60 per cent of households (NPC, 2011, p.326). The problem in South Africa is not one of

---

[56] In the UK, the Chancellor was forced to backtrack on a hugely unpopular decision to remove the formerly universal child benefit to any family in which there was someone earning over £50 000 per annum. Instead, the benefit will now be tapered at the rate of one per cent for every £100 earned over the threshold. Although this is an improvement over the original cliff edge at £50 000, at which point all benefits would be lost, it is still anomalous, in that a household with two earners each bringing in £49 000 per annum would still qualify for the benefit, whereas a household with a single earner on £60 000 per annum would lose it all. This points to the stupidity of means-tested benefits as opposed to universal – clawing back the 'surplus' through the tax system would obviate such unfairness. See the article "Budget 2012: pulling back from child benefit cliff edge still leaves dangers", by Randeep Ramesh and Hilary Osborne in the *Guardian*, 21 March 2012.
[57] The article "Sick infants not much better off than in ancient Sparta", by Paul Hoffman in *Business Day*, 16 July 2012, sub-titled "The situation in the public health sector is grossly improper, unconstitutional and illegal" provides a horrifying insight into the realities of clinical practice in South Africa. Because of a shortage of ICU beds, doctors in state hospitals are forced every day 'to play God' by sending back to general wards, critically ill infants for whom no ICU beds are available. This is a direct violation of the Bill of Rights in the country's constitution – children's rights to medical care are untrammelled by the 'weasel clause' in the Bill that allows government to wriggle out of its responsibility by resorting to the 'within available resources' excuse. The wider story is one of individuals and NGOs repeatedly challenging government on issues of accountability.

discovering who is deprived – rather, it is one of delivering what has been promised. In short, almost every one of the deprivations with which Alkire and her colleagues are concerned is taken into account.

But enough now of that – to bring the section to a close, let us reflect for a moment on the stomach-churning nature of the 'weighting' process involved in creating the MPI. Cast in mathematical terms, weighting looks neutral and benign. Consider the simple composite index described in formal terms in the expression below. Here, "C_i is the composite score for system i, P_{ij} is the individual measure for attribute j in system i, and α_i is the weight attached to attribute j".

$$C_i = \alpha_1 P_{i1} + \alpha_2 P_{i2} + \cdots + \alpha_n P_{in} = \sum_j \alpha_j P_{ij} \ldots\ldots\ldots \text{(Smith, 2002, p.297)}$$

As Smith points out, the weights are intended "… to indicate the relative importance of the indicators". If the problem of transforming or rescaling indicators is ignored, then "… the ratio α_1 / α_2 indicates the sacrifice in objective 2 that the user is prepared to make in order to gain an extra unit of objective 1." (Smith, 2002, p.305). When translated from the elegance of mathematics into everyday speech, naïve readers are jolted (or should be jolted) rapidly into reality. Martin Ravallion's statement of the same proposition in prose goes like this:

> "It is not credible to contend that any single index could capture all that matters in all settings. No consensus exists on what dimensions to include and how they should be weighted to form the composite index. *We can all agree that reducing child mortality is a hugely important development goal, but how can one contend—as the Alkire-Santos index does, for example—that avoiding the death of a child is equivalent to alleviating the combined deprivations of having a dirt floor, cooking with wood,[58] and not having a radio, TV, telephone, bike or car? Or that attaining these material conditions is equivalent to an extra year of schooling or to not have any malnourished family member?* These are difficult judgments to make. Thankfully resolving all such tradeoffs is not commonly needed in policy making at the country level. But when one faces a tradeoff, because a policy spans more than one dimension, those with a stake in the outcomes will almost certainly be in a better position to determine what weights to apply than the analyst calibrating a measure of poverty. The specific country and policy context should determine what tradeoff is considered appropriate.

---

[58] It could be argued that cooking with paraffin (kerosene) in informal townships is more hazardous by far than with wood and is hence a better indicator of deprivation. A study in South Africa shows that children living in squatter settlements perceive the fires (often caused by paraffin stoves) as the "… greatest threat to life and well-being in their neighbourhood." See Bray, 2010, p.118.

This will often be a political decision, though hopefully a well informed one." (Ravallion, 2011, pp.16-17, emphasis added)

Because fiscal and human resources are finite (scarce), policy-makers frequently face trade-offs of this nature. Being saddened at the thought does not reduce, let alone obviate the need for them to be made. Like Ravallion, one hopes (probably in vain), that such decisions will be well-informed, and that the voices of those most affected will be heard.

Mismatches: A back-of-envelop check

Moved by the frequent use of income poverty as a guide to anti-poverty policy, Alkire and Santos conduct an analysis that reveals (i) exclusion errors (deserving households that do not receive benefits), and (ii) inclusion errors (non-deserving households that do receive benefits) when income poverty measures are the criterion (2010a, p.41). They do this by cross-tabulating the four possible outcomes of a comparison between MPIs and income poverty estimates – poor by both measures; not poor by both measures; MPI poor and income non-poor; and income poor and non-MPI poor.[59] By examining the results of the 19 countries for which this type of comparison was possible (essentially countries whose results are drawn from the World Health Surveys (WHSs), Alkire and Santos manage to uncover a pattern which suggests that:

"… the exclusion error (percentage of people who are not income poor but MPI poor) is higher for poorer countries, whereas the inclusion error (percentage of people who are income poor but not MPI poor) is higher for less poor countries. It may be worth recalling that the poverty estimates of South Africa, Guatemala, Sri Lanka, Tunisia, the Russian Federation, and Latvia should be seen as lower bounds. This may explain part of the inclusion error." (2010a, p.43)

If I am reading this correctly, what the last sentence appears to suggest is that part of the reason why the 'inclusion error' in the South African MPI is high, may be found in the fact that it is a 'less poor' poor country. The proposition, cautiously advanced, reads thus:

"Admittedly these results are indicative only, especially because the consumption module is abbreviated in WHS (*sic*). However they do suggest that income becomes a poorer proxy for MPI among high poverty countries, perhaps

---

[59] South Africa, with its low MPI headcount and its high $1.25/day headcount, would be approaching the 'income poor and non-MPI poor' category.

in part because income does not capture access to basic services." (Alkire and Santos, 2010a, p.43)

There is some resonance in this argument with the standard government response to claims by critics that poverty in South Africa was not being effectively tackled, which was to point out that the income poverty measures used to draw this conclusion failed to take account of what they call the 'social wage' – essentially, health care, education, subsidised housing, and a variety of utility services such as a free basic allowance of water and electricity.[60] Hundreds of demonstrations and protests (often violent) about the poor quality of services by those affected have occasionally taught government a lesson in manners. Official response, however, to gross bureaucratic incompetence and corruption, is, I fear, nowhere near strong enough to address the storm of discontent.

Be all that as it may, let us see if a little back-of-envelope calculation can tell us anything about inclusion error. As we shall see below in Table 2, the total monthly expenditure of about 28.5 per cent of South Africa's population was reported to have been below the food poverty line in 2000. By the year 2006, the proportion had fallen to 24.8 per cent. It does not seem outrageous to assume that the value for 2003, the year for which Alkire and Santos estimate the MPI, the proportion would have been about 26 per cent. If individuals near the line spent every cent on food, they could possibly satisfy the Alkire and Santos nutrition criterion (Nutrition – If any adult or child in the family is malnourished). Since people cannot live by food alone, nearly everyone at or below the food line must have been malnourished. Score 16.66 per cent in the MPI box.

For education, Alkire and Santos settle upon:

- "Years of Schooling – If no household member has completed 5 years schooling
- Child school attendance – If any school-aged child is out of school in years 1-8"

Ignore that choice and specify instead 'education quality' (a characteristic they recognise as important but not one that they are able to measure). Accept on trust, for the moment, the claim that the quality of education in 80 per cent of schools is so bad that the schools may validly be labelled 'dysfunctional' (Bergman et al, 2011). Accept as well that pupils in the country's poorest provinces do least well at school.

[60] See Meth (2008) for an overview of the debate, a critique of the government position, and for suggestions of ways to address, partially, the intractable problems of valuing government expenditure.

The odds are that nearly every child in households eking out an existence on an income that is lower than the food poverty line will be deprived by virtue of the poor quality of the education they receive – an 'education' that probably consigns them permanently to the bottom rungs of society, assuming in the first place that they had the stamina to receive that education. Score another 16.66 per cent in the MPI box. By these calculations, at least a quarter of South Africa's population in 2003 would have been MPI poor – the 2003 'lower bound' of three per cent found by Alkire and Santos is a joke.

In setting out to create the international league table for the 2010 HDR, Alkire and Santos made two fundamental errors. The first was to use a 'one-size-fits-all' approach to the selection of indicators for education and health, presumably so they could tick one of the 'pro' boxes on the list compiled by Joumard *et al* (2011) reproduced above, namely that of 'facilitating the task of benchmarking countries'. In doing so, they fall into the 'con' trap of 'inviting simplistic policy conclusions that may lead to inappropriate policies if dimensions of performance that are difficult to measure are ignored or poorly represented'. It will be many decades before 'Health' in South Africa (and probably several other countries as well), can be measured adequately by trying to count the number of dead children.

The second error was to tighten the already tight constraint on the choice of data source facing them – once again, possibly to 'facilitate the task of benchmarking countries' by keeping to a minimum, the number of different surveys used. The decision to use the WHS, a small, albeit carefully crafted survey, ensured (at least in South Africa's case), that estimates of the poorly chosen indicators for education and health, which make up two thirds of the MPI, would probably sit inside a confidence interval large enough to accommodate a Routemaster bus. As noted above, the switch to the much larger NIDS database for the 2011 HDR (the 2008 MPI), and the fourfold increase in the number of multi-dimensionally poor it caused, shows just how wrong it was to place any faith in the WHS. Instead of merely attaching the label 'lower bound' to the 2003 South African MPI (the absence of an upper bound is significant); they should, in their analysis of mismatches, have devoted more attention to the possibility (and consequences) of indicator failure.

Competition below the radar? The MPI and the IMD

Among the people thanked by Alkire and Santos for their "very useful comments" on the MPI are Michael Noble and Gemma Wright (Alkire and Santos, 2010a, p.3), respectively, director and deputy-director of the Centre for the Analysis of South African Social Policy (CASASP) in the University of Oxford. CASASP's website describes OPHI, the institution that produces the MPI, as an 'academic partner', saying that CASASP "works closely with OPHI". Given this, it is more than a little odd that in the papers in which the properties and virtues of the MPI are canvassed, I have found only a single reference to measures of the sort created by CASASP.[61] The measure, which sets out to do something similar to the MPI, is the Index of Multiple Deprivation (IMD).

In one of the first reports issued by the CASASP team (Noble *et al*, 2006a) reference is made to the constitutional requirement in South Africa that

"... financial resources [be] distributed equitably among provincial and sub-provincial governments, based partly on levels of poverty and disadvantage... "

From this is it is concluded that:

"It is therefore critical that robust measures are developed to quantify the nature and extent of social deprivation at sub-national level and thereby accurately identify the areas of greatest need (i.e. the most deprived areas)." (2006a, p.7)

The Index of Multiple Deprivation (IMD) is the measure intended to meet this requirement. Unlike the MPI, the IMD does not set out to measure the numbers of individuals suffering multiple deprivations. Nor does it attempt to establish a cutoff, below which people are defined as acutely poor because they suffer a multiplicity of deprivations. Rather, the CASASP people attempt to discover the extent of deprivation by area. Here is how they describe the process:

"At an area level it is difficult to measure the percentage of the population experiencing one, two or more deprivations. It is possible, however, to look at single deprivations at an area level and state that a certain proportion of the population experiences that deprivation, a proportion experiences some other form of deprivation etc., and at an area level describe the combination of single deprivations as area level multiple deprivation.

The area itself can be characterised as deprived relative to other areas, in a particular dimension of deprivation, on the basis of the proportion of people in the area experiencing the type of deprivation in question. Having attributed the aggregate of individual experience of deprivation to the area, it is possible to say that an area is deprived in that particular dimension. Once the specific dimensions of deprivation have been measured, these can be understood as elements of multiple deprivation." (Noble *et al*, 2006a, p.8)

---

[61] The reference, in Alkire (2011, p.76), is to work by Christopher Dibben, an associate (and former staff member) of CASASP.

The method by which they combine the single deprivations to form an index of multiple deprivation does not concern us here – suffice it to say that once area IMDs have been estimated, they can be ranked from least to most deprived.[62] The CASASP people isolate the deprived by reference to a set of indicators (as must all who play this game). It is not necessary to look at any of these until we get to the discussion below on health in South Africa.

Like Alkire *et al*, the CASASP people are data constrained. Rather than relying on small surveys like the WHS, the initial estimates of the IMD used South Africa's 2001 population census as the base on which to begin building. Instead of dimensions, Noble *et al* refer to the areas of deprivation as domains. There does not appear to be any reason in principle, however, why the census data cannot be analysed using the Alkire Foster (AF) method – after all, a census is nothing more than a very large survey that collects information on individuals grouped together in households, the basic unit of analysis for the MPI. Treating the household, as opposed to the geographical area, as unit of analysis, is the major difference between the MPI and the IMD.

For the first published set of IMD estimates, five domains were specified, namely:

- Income and material deprivation
- Employment
- Health
- Education
- Living environment

They also considered, but did not include, crime and social order, and proximity to social services. Of the number of potential applications of the IMD, Noble *et al* say that the major use to which it be put is to "assist with spatial targeting", that is to say, to:

"directing of programmes and resources within programmes towards those in greatest social need" (2006a, p.50)

Initially, IMDs based on the 2001 census (Noble *et al*, 2006a) were presented by province, rather than as a single national set, purportedly due to stark variations in

---

[62] The South African IMD builds "… on work undertaken by CASASP's sister research centre, the Social Disadvantage Research Centre (SDRC) in constructing national indices of deprivation at small area level" in the UK. See Noble *et al*, 2006a, p.11. For details of the UK IMD, see McLennan *et al*, 2011.

average ward size across provinces, meaning that if all wards were set alongside one another, provinces with large wards (such as Gauteng) would fail to be given fair prominence.

Recognising the limitations of this first foray, they single out several areas for further development. The most important of these relate to the need to measure deprivation in small, relatively homogeneous geographical areas, and the need to find means to update the IMDs. Electoral wards in South Africa, the smallest geographical unit used in the creation of their first IMD, varied in size from 150 to more than 80 000 people, hence the need to create a new geography of deprivation (Noble *et al*, 2006a, pp.53ff).

An opportunity for the CASASP team to update the IMDs (Wright and Noble, 2009) presented itself as a result of the massive Community Survey (274 000 households in the sample) conducted by Statistics South Africa in 2007, in lieu of the population census that was supposed to have taken place in 2006. Although the updated IMD estimates exclude the health domain (because the 2007 Community Survey did not gather the required data on mortality),[63] the report presented IMDs for the whole country at municipal level, instead of sealing the municipalities into their respective provinces. It could now be claimed with some justification that the IMDs were well on their way towards policy relevance at a national, as opposed to a provincial level.

Let us digress for a moment, to reflect on the nature of the relationship between policy relevance and the level of decomposition (disaggregation?) of a composite index like the MPI or the IMD.[64] Possibly the most important quality of the relationship is that the level of aggregation of the index or indicator should 'correspond' to the scope or magnitude of the policy issue in question.[65] Monetary

---

[63] Alkire and Santos performed estimations using the 2007 Community Survey (CS) but decided to use the WHS because the CS lacks nutrition information, and because the mortality data are inadequate (2010a, p.22n). Sadly, the fact that the survey is very large cannot automatically be taken to mean that it is reliable. This notwithstanding, use has been made of the CS by Sartorius *et al* (2011) to construct a spatial analysis of excess infant mortality at a sub-district level. The resulting distributions bear a more than passing resemblance to the mapping of multiple deprivation produced by Noble *et al* (2010, p.15).

[64] So irritated was I at the blanket claim of policy relevance that Alkire *et al* made for the MPI, that it felt reasonable, in the face of the manifest absence of this quality in the South African estimate, to request from them a clear statement of what they thought policy relevance meant. On reflection, such a demand is clearly unreasonable – policy relevant indicators come in all shapes and sizes.

[65] Below provincial level, South Africa's General Household Surveys, with a sample size of 30 000 households, cannot be relied upon to produce evidence suitable for addressing acute multiple deprivation.

policy, conducted at national level (with international constraints) is quite happy with M1 or M2 or whatever. A development project conducted at village level clearly needs specially created local indicators.

With this in mind, hark back to the list of claims made above for what the MPI can do, in particular, to this item:

- **"Target the poorest groups and beneficiaries of conditional cash transfers, district interventions or public programmes**. The targetting tool can be broken down to show the indicators in which they are most deprived."

This subject, it will be recalled, was addressed above with reference to the BPL census in India, designed to identify social assistance beneficiaries. 'District interventions', although not as data hungry as locating individual beneficiaries, would still, one imagines, require fine grained measures, measures that depend for their creation on national surveys, or comprehensive area specific surveys. Noble *et al* have made some progress in this direction. In 2009, CASASP published IMDs for the whole country at data zone level ("small area level statistical geographical units"), based once again on the 2001 census data (Noble *et al*, 2009). This was updated to a 2007 time point, using the 2007 Community Survey (Noble, Dibben and Wright, 2010). There were about 22 000 data zones, with average populations of 2100 or so. Since data do not exist at the requisite level, resort has to be had to modeling techniques to derive the desired results for 2007. The method used to achieve this is described briefly on pp. 10ff of the paper. Although there is considerable overlap with the deprivation maps produced at national level (2010, p.10), their conclusions are suitably modest – the results, they say, are plausible, but must be treated as experimental, for want of any other small area data to use to validate them (2010, p.26). If the arguments against universal grants, and in favour of rationed (means-tested) benefits are accepted (and it is by no means clear that this contentious manner of distributing benefits and services is optimal), then some device targeting potential benefit recipients is required. Suitably refined, knowledge gained of deprivation at data zone level could be of use in addressing the targeting problem that has always to be faced benefits of this sort are contemplated.

Mindful of the warning by Alkire and Foster (2011) not to launch a critique of the MPI in general for its use of data in particular cases, we can still safely conclude that if they want the MPI to contribute to the task of 'targeting the poor .... at district level', (or even at municipal level) they will have to solve the same problems as Noble *et al*. In the process, they will they have to address the fact that even relatively small geographical areas contain households of widely differing degrees of deprivation (Elbers *et al*, 2004). The larger the area, the greater the likelihood that both inclusion and exclusion errors will occur, and the greater the need for supplementary data sources and information to assist in the business of targeting.[66]

It seems fitting to end this section with a disclaimer, namely, that it is obviously silly to deny the importance of doing the best that can possibly be done to measure poverty in a multi-dimensional manner. The policy relevance of doing so is obvious – South Africa is a federal state – the constitution requires that provinces receive equitable shares of nationally raised revenue. The basis on which allocation takes place is specified in a formula that takes account of 'real' conditions (but poverty reduction is not an aim). This is discussed in an excellent paper by Basarir (2011), which, using South Africa's 30 000 household General Household Survey for 2007 as data source, examines the different rankings at provincial level produced by a variety of approaches (including the AF) to measuring multi-dimensional poverty.[67] Testing existing and alternative distribution mechanisms for conformity with different notions of social justice could potentially make a valuable contribution to the debate about poverty and inequality in South Africa.[68] But enough now of this – let us look at some of the simpler calculations that Alkire and Santos had to make in 2010, and the confusion that arose from their attempt to do so.

---

[66] The literature on targeting is huge (and enticing). The piece by Elbers *et al* (2004) shows the differences that can be made to poverty alleviation using poverty maps of the sort created by Noble *et al*, identifying in the process the problems that have still to be solved. Another fascinating and controversial avenue (down which we shall not travel) is that of participatory budgeting (Schneider and Goldfrank, 2002; Shah (ed), 2007)

[67] The piece contains no reference to the 2010a Alkire and Santos paper.

[68] The topic is a minefield – a recent paper by Leibbrandt *et al* (2011), one, incidentally, that steers clear of theories of social justice, sees the authors raising, then tiptoeing around some highly contentious topics, e.g., rewarding teachers for their role in the struggle to remove racial salary disparities, but at such a cost as to place severe limits on further spending on education (p.17). Their strong emphasis on the need to tackle both inequality and poverty, and the extreme difficulties of reducing the former (p.15), points to a weakness of the MPI, one it shares with its stablemate, the FGT Pα poverty measures, namely, an inability to say much about inequality (Meth, 2011, pp.16ff).

Section 3 The MPI and other odd South African results

Sometimes, when a perceptive outsider looks at one's country, the freshness of their gaze offers insights or opens vistas that one's own jaded eye overlooks – good travel writers have this gift. Sadly, good economics 'travel' writers are not numerous. In the old days in South Africa, a standard joke about National Party politicians (the apartheid ruling group), usually uttered out of earshot of their thugs, was that their bizarre perceptions of reality arose because they were so narrow-minded, they could look through a keyhole with both eyes. A contemporary equivalent would have Alkire and Santos visiting the country on their laptops, squinting at it through a narrow, irregular grid placed over a lens specially ground to cause astigmatism, then making a pronouncement whose value did not differ much from zero (it is not unfair to say that it was probably negative). Having omitted to tell the outfit who broadcast the findings (the UNDP), to give the South Africans a health warning, one imagines them wending their way to the next triumph over the uni-dimensionals, minds filled with axioms and dreams of theoretical rigour and empirical robustness.

Left behind them, however, was a small addition to the mess among the income poverty estimates that needs to be cleared up before further progress became possible. As noted above, by changing survey sources, they have made some amends for the rubbish they dumped into the pool called 'policy relevant' research. It is a pity that they have not drawn attention to this little episode. As was also noted above, there is a sense in which the error is a blessing – had it not been the case that the 2003 MPI was so obviously wrong – had the estimates seemed vaguely plausible, it is possible that the thing could have escaped scrutiny altogether (life is short and there are more amusing things to do), which would have meant that the errors still present in the MPI estimates would probably have escaped attention.

In order to uncover the mistakes in the 2003 MPI for South Africa, it was necessary to act like an auditor's clerk. Those without the stomach (heart?) to wade through the dreary pages that follow, are welcome to skip to the next section, safe in the knowledge that not only have the Alkire and Santos estimates dissected below, i.e., those given in the 2010 HDR been superceded by the somewhat more plausible MPI estimates that appeared in the 2011 HDR, but also that most of the income poverty estimates considered below do not inspire much confidence, anyway. It is possible that the estimates made by Statistics South Africa, the country's official statistics producer, were (are) somewhere near the 'truth' of the matter, but of that we cannot be assured.

When major differences arise between the 'official' figures and estimates such as those produced by Alkire and Santos, it would be comforting if the agents of an international institution like the UNDP took the pains to discover why the figures they publish disagree with those put out by the government concerned. Where large discrepancies exist and cannot be reconciled, user's attention should be drawn to the disagreement. Even if income poverty estimates from the two sources can be forced into alignment, it must, however, still be stressed that the mere act of doing so can offer no guarantee that the estimates are 'correct'. Suitably armed, let us look into the mess made by the 2010 Alkire and Santos figure.

To reduce cacophony levels when constructing international league tables of certain welfare variables, ways have to be found to navigate around a number of well-known obstacles. Among uni-dimensional poverty estimates, rendering income and/or expenditure comparable between countries, is one of the most formidable. One procedure adopted is to convert the values of these variables expressed in national currencies to PPP (purchasing power parity) dollars. To do this, resort must be had to conversion factors furnished by the arbiter of these matters, the World Bank (with assistance from several other institutions). Estimates of poverty rates and implied headcounts in Table 2 below are based on poverty lines expressed in PPP dollars.

It is not possible for all of the poverty headcount ratios in the table to be correct – it could be, as noted above, that all, or several of them are incorrect, and if not incorrect, based upon so parsimonious a poverty line as to be meaningless. At first glance, one of the explanations that suggested itself for at least part of the clashes among the estimates, was that the estimates were based on different PPP conversion factors.[69] A little diffident about asserting outright that the survey from which Alkire and Santos concocted their 2003 MPI was wholly unsuited to the task, I waffled on about the PPP source that they cite (it is on pp.41-42 of the 2010 paper), then observed that Statistics South Africa (Stats SA), in the official report to the UNDP (produced with financial support from that organisation) from which the figures in Table 2 are drawn, must be using a different PPP conversion factor,[70] and/or a different set of household expenditure data from which to extract poverty

---

[69] When last I looked at the PPP in any detail (Meth, 2007b, pp.25ff), the tired set of estimates based on benchmarks created in 1993 were assailed on all sides. South Africa had not been one of the 'benchmark' countries, so it relied for its PPP rate on an extrapolation. It was not known how good (or bad) this was. Revised PPPs were published after the International Comparison Program completed the re-benchmarking to the year 2005 (World Bank, 2008). The PPP conversions now available are as good as they going to get for a while, although trouble caused by the international financial crisis is looming (McCarthy, 2011).

[70] Problems with PPP estimates and the $1.25/day line are discussed further below in Footnote No. 71.

estimates.[71] Sample sizes for the two Income and Expenditure Surveys (IESs) used by Stats SA were 30 000 households in each case, as opposed to the 2528 interviewed out of 3157 selected in the 2003 WHS (WHO, 2003, p13). The statement thereafter in Versions 1 and 2 of the paper that it did not follow as a matter of course that bigger is better, because Stats SA is known to have had problems with both IESs, may be a gratuitous insult – maybe the Stats SA estimates are roughly 'correct', but then again, maybe not.

Table 2 consists of three panels. The first (Rows 1-4) contains two poverty headcount rate estimates drawn from Alkire and Santos, the MPI rate and the income poverty rate for the year 2003 based on the 'national' poverty line for South Africa estimated by the World Bank. It also presents two headcount rate estimates for which figures from Statistics South Africa, albeit for different years, are available. To permit a comparison between these latter figures and the Alkire and Santos figures, estimates for 2003 have been made by linear interpolation from the 2000 and 2006 Stats SA results. Panel 2 (Rows 5-7) presents Statistics South Africa estimates of the food poverty rates in 2000 and 2006. Once again, linear interpolation is applied to obtain an estimate for 2003. The third panel (Rows 8-9) presents the poverty headcounts implied by the rates in panels 1 and 2.

Alkire and Santos use a total population figure of 49.2 million for 2007 (2010a, Table 1.4, p.96). Statistics South Africa thought that the mid-year population in 2003 was 46.4 million (Statistical release P0302, 24 July 2003, p.6), and that the total population only reached 49.3 million in 2009 (Statistical release P0302, 27 July 2009, p.4). Row 8 shows the effects of using one or the other of the two population estimates. The differences, if they were real, would be a matter of concern for poor people. And so, to the results themselves – the MPI headcount rate of 3.1 per cent (Row 1) implies a headcount of 1.4-1.5 million people suffering multi-dimensional poverty (Row 8). The Alkire and Santos finding that 26 per cent of the South African population 'enjoyed' daily consumption levels of $1.25/day or less, translates to about 12.2-12.9 million people. As may be seen, the $1.25 line generates roughly the same headcount rate as South Africa's food poverty line (the line itself being another contentious matter which we must address). The Alkire and Santos figure of 26.2 per cent thus implied that those concerned did not have sufficient income to purchase the food required to subsist, let alone anything else. How was it possible to reconcile this with the finding that a mere three per cent of the population met the criteria for inclusion among the MPI poor?

---

[71] Statistics South Africa used the Income and Expenditure Surveys (IESs) conducted in 2000 and 2006 respectively. For a summary of the main findings see Stats SA, 2002 and Stats SA, 2008.

Table 2 South Africa: MPI poor and income poor (various poverty lines)

Panel 1				Income poverty headcount rates (%)			
Row		Year	MPI head-count rate (%)	$1.25/day	$2/day	National poverty line	
1	Alkire & Santos	2003	3.1	26.2	42.9	22.0	
2	Statistics SA	2000		17.0	33.5		
3		2006		9.7	25.3		
4	Interpolated Stats SA estimate	2003		13.4	29.4		
Panel 2				Food poverty headcount rates (%)			
5	Statistics SA	2000					28.5
6		2006					24.8
7	Interpolated Stats SA estimate	2003					26.7
Panel 3				Implied headcounts (millions)			
			MPI poor	$1.25/day	$2/day	National poverty line	Food poverty
8	Alkire and Santos headcounts (millions)	2007	1.5	12.9	21.1	10.8	
		2003	1.4	12.2	19.9	10.2	
9	Interpolated Stats SA estimate	2003		6.2	13.6		12.4

Sources: Alkire and Santos, 2010a, pp.74 and 96; and Statistics South Africa *MDG Country Report 2010* (Stats SA, 2011a, pp.24 and 29).
Note: Rand/PPP dollar conversions are given on p.128 of the *MDG Country Report 2010*. The 2007 headcount estimates in Row 8 are obtained using the Alkire and Santos population estimate of 49.2 million in 2007. The 2003 estimates use the Stats SA population estimate of 46.4 million.

Alkire's and Santos' reference to a 'national' poverty line for South Africa sent me on a bit of a wild goose chase in Version 1 of the paper. The account of that chase offered here has been allowed to stand because the debate in South Africa (actually, absence of debate) about a 'proper' national poverty line is something of a problem.

Ten minute's reading of, say, Chen and Ravallion (2009) would have dissolved my ignorance about the 'national poverty line' to which Alkire and Santos refer. That 'national' line, however, has little or nothing to do with the problem of the absence of a domestically agreed poverty line, a topic to which we shall turn further below. Getting back to international poverty lines, I must say that much as I enjoy some of Martin Ravallion's work, I am allergic to applications of the $1.25/day 'starvation' line, both in South Africa and elsewhere. It took me a while, therefore, to work out that the 'national' poverty line to which Alkire and Santos were referring had nothing to do with an official poverty line of domestic provenance, but rather to an external thing devised by the World Bank and imposed (if that is not too harsh a word, and it may not be) on developing countries.

The route to finding out took a detour via the old Reddy and Pogge (2005) vs. Martin Ravallion debate on how good or bad the World Bank's income poverty estimates were, to the Chen and Ravallion (2009) paper.[72] The way in which 'national' poverty lines are estimated is described on p.5 of Reddy and Pogge (2005), and at greater length in Chen and Ravallion (2009). Precisely what the thing is supposed to measure is not clear to me, suffice it to say that according to the Row 1 figures in Table 2, it yields a poverty headcount ratio of 22 per cent, which must mean that it is less generous even than the $1.25/day line. The outcome is that whereas some 12-13 million people were to be found subsisting on less than the

---

[72] Reddy and Pogge took no prisoners – the beginning of the abstract of Version 6.2 (2005) of their paper reads thus: "The World Bank's approach to estimating the extent, distribution and trend of global income poverty is neither meaningful nor reliable. The Bank uses an arbitrary international poverty line that is not adequately anchored in any specification of the real requirements of human beings. Moreover, it employs a concept of purchasing power "equivalence" that is neither well defined nor appropriate for poverty assessment. These difficulties are inherent in the Bank's "money-metric" approach and cannot be credibly overcome without dispensing with this approach altogether." Ravallion's 2002 paper addressed Version 3.0 of the Reddy and Pogge attack. Who 'won', is not obvious – the continued popularity of the $1.25 line and its stablemates, along with the 'national' lines, suggests that it was the Bank. The storm, however, has not abated. Nothing daunted, Reddy (2008) returned to the struggle when the Chen and Ravallion (2009) paper came out in its 2008 guise. As before, he was dismissive of the PPPs and the $1.25 poverty line. A hard-hitting paper by Fischer (2010) about the poverty of poverty lines is very rude about the Chen and Ravallion effort – labelling their findings about poverty in China "a politically convenient narrative" (p.38).

meagre sum of $1.25/day, use of the 'national' poverty line reduced this to some 10.2-10.8 million people (Row 8). Why it should be thought appropriate to estimate a 'national' poverty line, which when used, generates lower poverty headcount rates than a food poverty line devised in the same country – 22 per cent (Row 1) vs. approximately 27 per cent (Row 7) with correspondingly lower headcounts (Rows 8 and 9) is by no means clear. Allowing such implausible results to be published without comment is negligent.

Look now at the grey-highlighted Alkire and Santos 2010a results in Row 1 and the corresponding interpolated Stats SA figures in Row 4 (assume that the values in Row 4 are valid approximations of a 2003 poverty headcount ratio estimate). Plainly, there was a major disagreement on the extent of extreme poverty in South Africa. At the $1.25/day line, the Stats SA figure suggest that income poverty in South Africa was only half as severe as Alkire and Santos suggest it was (headcounts of 6 vs. 12-13 million in Rows 9 and 8). Below the $2/day line, Stats SA find less than 30 per cent of the population – Alkire and Santos have almost 43 per cent of people below this level. Corresponding headcounts are 20-21 million for Alkire and Santos (Row 8) as opposed to 13.6 million for the interpolated figure for Stats SA (Row 9). The 2008 MPI changes all of this – now the Alkire *et al* estimate of the $1.25/day poverty headcount rate is down to 17.4 per cent, while that at the 'national' poverty line is 23 per cent, implying that the latter is higher than the former.[73]

Let us leave the Table 2 results for the meanwhile and move to something that I described in Versions 1 and 2 of the paper as equally contentious, but not quite as messy – the disaggregated MPI estimates. A set of tables at the end of the Alkire and Santos paper provide details of the final numbers that go into the making of the MPI. For our purposes, the table of most interest gives 'the percentage of the population with at least one severe deprivation in *n*, i.e., the raw proportion of the population deprived in *n*, where *n* is one of the the three MPI dimensions they have chosen. Estimates of this variable for South Africa are given in panel 1 of Table 3 below.[74] In panel 2, estimates of the percentage contribution of each of the

---

[73] This reversal goes some way towards undoing the implausibility of the earlier effort.

[74] Alkire and Santos also estimate 'Censored headcounts' with which "… one can prioritize the poorest poor and provide the basis for further policy analysis that may find effective ways of reducing deprivation in one indicator by improving some other." The censored headcounts "…reflect the percentage of people who are poor and deprived in each indicator. These differ from traditional headcounts in two ways. In the first place, they are the proportion of population that are poor (i.e., deprived in some combination of two to six indicators) *and* deprived in each indicator." Lest anyone be tempted to marvel at the tiny value these headcounts take, Alkire and Santos point out that: "It is worth re-emphasizing that as a consequence of the … differences between our censored headcounts and the

dimensions to the MPI are given. It may seem a trifle odd that the dimension in which deprivation is least widely distributed in the population as a whole, contributes most to the MPI. This is resolved as soon as one recalls that in order to be classed as MPI poor, the individuals concerned must experience deprivation caused by "some combination of indicators whose weighted sum is 30 percent or more of the dimensions" (Alkire and Santos, 2010a, p.7).

It is even more convincingly resolved when one compares the distribution of the 'pie' of contributions to the 2003 MPI in Figure 1 above with the corresponding values in Figure 2. The Figure 1 distribution is repeated in the lower panel of Table 3. It is no longer necessary now to describe the 2003 distribution as 'contentious' – it is merely wrong, something disclosed not by an admission of its wrongness by Alkire and Santos, but rather by their switch to a better set of survey results.

If the raw headcount estimates were to be believed, then a mere three per cent of the country's population, by their definition, would have suffered a severe deprivation in education, with eight per cent being severely deprived in the health dimension. Results like that cannot but cause those familiar with the education and health sectors in South Africa, to raise an eyebrow. The figure for severe deprivations in living standards is a little higher – but with 26 per cent of the population below the $1.25/day line and 43 per cent below the $2/day line, according to Alkire and Santos (2010a) and the 2010 HDR, that could scarcely have come as a surprise.

Table 3 South Africa's 2003 MPI disaggregated into dimensions and indicators

Panel 1. Raw proportion of population with at least one severe deprivation in … (%)		
Education	Health	Living standards
3.2	8.1	10.8
Source: Alkire and Santos, 2010a, Table 1.9, p.113.		
Panel 2. Contribution of deprivations to MPI (%)		
Education	Health	Living standards
57.84	11.72	30.44
Source: Alkire and Santos, 2010a, Table 1.3, p.86.		
Note: In Table 1.9 Alkire and Santos repeat the warning that: "The poverty estimates for [South Africa] should be interpreted as lower bound estimates, meaning that multidimensional poverty is at least as great as their MPI values indicates." (2010a, p.115)		

traditional ones, the headcounts on nutrition, mortality, education, and school attendance should not be compared with standard measures of these variables reported elsewhere by different organizations." (2010a, pp.28-29).

In Versions 1 and 2 of the present paper, I speculated that if South Africa's food poverty line (on which, more below) was somewhere near a modest $1.72/day, then by the results in Table 2, it was possible that somewhere in the region of 25-30 per cent of the population was seriously malnourished, because they were seriously income deprived. How one would square that with the 11 per cent of the population in Table 3 who are said to suffer at least one severe deprivation in living standards, was not immediately obvious. But enough now of the travails of the MPI for South Africa and its collision with the South African poverty estimates – it is time to spend some time looking at the peculiarities of some of the poverty lines used above.

Which poverty lines, if any, can we trust?

There is nothing like a good polemic to get the juices flowing. Most critics of the estimators of uni-dimensional (income or expenditure) poverty measures, chide the measurers (usually economists) relatively gently for neglecting the multi-dimensional nature of poverty, before setting out to make their own contribution to the debate.[75] Saith (2005) is much more robust – it is worth quoting a passage from his work at some length to illustrate the strength of his feelings on the matter. Here he is in full flight:

> "…. it is not enough to say that [poverty] is all around us; we as academics and policy makers, have an almost existential need to know precisely how much of "it" there is, and who "they" are, and what impact anti-poverty interventions might have had on "them". Here there is a clash of disciplinary cultures, with economists who tend to dominate with their ostensibly more usable forms of knowledge – a self-made and self-verified claim. And this opens the door to much sophistication and sophistry as specialists set about reducing poverty and the poor to their uni-scalar quantifiable core, viz., those below the so-called poverty line reckoned in money metric terms. In this, they acknowledge, but then immediately ignore[76] and exclude, the essential multi-dimensionality and the relational nature of the lived experiences of deprivation." (2005, p.2)

---

[75] With customary elegance, Kanbur (2009) condenses most of the major criticisms of conventional income poverty measurement into five pages.

[76] Not all of us do this all the time. My 2008 paper on poverty and the social wage, engaged at length with government expenditure and its impact on poverty, while my 2011 paper on how not to present poverty research results contains detailed pro-forma recommendations on income poverty measurement, intended to supplement the meagre Foster-Greer-Thorbecke (FGT) estimates. So often, the FGTs are presented simply as a set of point estimates of P_0, P_1 and P_2 – sometimes readers are not even offered the gift of a set of headcounts, let alone estimates of what it would cost to close the poverty gap. This, of course, is not the fault of Foster, Greer and Thorbecke – it is sloppiness on the part of the researchers concerned.

Stirring stuff, and of course all too true! Unless, however, the many serious problems still facing the multi-dimensional brigade (some discussed in the present paper) are solved, it is likely that closing down the uni-scalar business would leave us (academics, policy makers and the poor themselves) unable to say much about the scale and intensity of poverty at the macro-level, where some of the big decisions about how to combat income poverty have to be made. Conventional uni-dimensional poverty measures may only vouchsafe us the vaguest outline of the extent of poverty. That, though, may be enough to prompt government to act – South Africa's Child Support Grant, now reaching almost 11 million children, is possibly a case in point. The position taken here is that whatever their drawbacks (and they are many), carefully estimated (sensitivity tested) income poverty measures are better than none at all, especially if the only other available measures are weak multi-dimensional indices – imagine if the South African government were forced to rely on the 2003 and 2008 MPIs produced by Alkire and her colleagues.

Suitably humbled, let us scratch around a little more in the poverty figures. At first glance, the Stats SA poverty estimates in Table 2 apparently possess the virtue of consistency. Poverty is lowest at the meanest poverty line ($1.25/day), less so at the food poverty line, and highest at the $2.00/day line. Something, however, is amiss – converting the $2/day figures into Rands, the local currency, gives figures of R167 in 2000, and R208 in 2006 (Stats SA, 2011a, p.128). Corresponding poverty headcount ratios are 33.5 and 25.3 per cent. The food poverty line, according to Statistics South Africa, was set at R148 in 2000, and R209 in 2006 (Stats SA, 2011a, p.28). To these figures corresponded poverty headcount rates of 28.5 and 24.8 per cent. How is it possible, the inquisitive reader may ask, for different poverty rates to be generated by almost identical poverty lines?

Versions 1 and 2 of the paper took us behind the scenes to see if it was possible to make sense of the poverty line situation. Clearly, making that journey is still necessary, because there is something decidedly odd going on. My understanding of the poverty line debate in South Africa was that the country's food poverty line (unofficial, but apparently blessed until recently by the authorities) was R211 per capita per month (in 2000 prices),[77] which looks, using the Statistics South Africa Rand/PPP$ conversion rate, as though it would have been in the region of PPP $2.50/day. It comes as something of a surprise, therefore, to discover that Statistics South Africa has put the value of the food poverty line at R148 per capita per month

---

[77] According to the *MDG Country Report*, PPP$2.50 was equal to about R215 in 2000 prices (Stats SA, 2011a, p.128).

in 2000 prices (about PPP $1.72/day).[78] In the fullness of time (when the complete results of Statistics South Africa's Living Conditions Survey are published), all may be revealed; then again, maybe not.

Debates about national poverty lines in South Africa, reach back a long way into history. The conversation took on renewed urgency when the contents of a paper by Babita *et al* (2003) – to the best of my knowledge, still unpublished – entered the public domain. The Babita *et al* effort resulted from an attempt by a team, put together by Statistics South Africa, to establish a national poverty line. One of the members of the team, on secondment from the World Bank, went ahead with a colleague and published the mooted figures (Hoogeveen and Özler, 2005 – earlier versions of the paper also circulated). Using a 'cost-of-basic-needs approach', Hoogeveen and Özler proposed a poverty range with a lower bound of R322 and an upper bound of R593 per capita per month (in 2000 prices). This was related to a food poverty line of R211 per capita per month, which they noted, was not far from a $2/day poverty line, the equivalent, according to their estimates, of about R174 per capita per month (2005, p.7).

It seemed as though the Hoogeveen and Özler (alias Babita *et al*) figures had gained fairly wide acceptance. A joint paper by the National Treasury and Statistics South Africa discussed the R211 food poverty line and its companion, the R322 line, and mentioned the R593 line as well (National Treasury, 2007, pp.7-9).[79] The paper's authors also spoke about an 'extreme poverty line', referring to the occasional use of the $2/day line (about R162 per capita per month in 2000 prices, by their calculations) to measure that state (p.9). The text's authors stop short of proposing this as the marker for the lower threshold of poverty. The draft proposal in the joint Treasury/Statistics South Africa paper called for: "A single national poverty line based on minimum food needs for daily energy requirements, plus essential non-food items, calculated on a simple per capita basis", and "Two additional thresholds below and above the poverty line as indicators of extreme poverty and of a broader level of household income adequacy" (2007, p.10).

Progress thereafter was glacial – in the 2009 national budget vote for Statistics South Africa, under the heading "Measuring poverty", the following statement appears:

---

[78] This value is obtained by interpolation from the PPP/Rand exchange rates given on p.128 of Stats SA, 2011a. There are two ways of performing the calculation – the other method yields a figure of $1.77. It is not obvious whether $1.77 or $1.72 should be used in the argument. For our purposes here, the difference does not appear to be significant.
[79] For a trenchant critique of the use of food poverty as the basis for estimating poverty lines, see Saith (2005, pp.6ff).

"In line with international best practice, the use of an official poverty line has been proposed for South Africa to measure the extent of household poverty and monitor progress in poverty reduction. Statistics South Africa is currently conducting a living conditions survey designed to measure poverty, using a multidimensional approach, and statistical information on South Africa's poverty profile will be released in 2010." (National Treasury, 2009, p.205)

The first of the living conditions survey (LCS) reports has been published. It refers several times to 'poverty line', see, for example, p.74 in Statistical release P0310, 15 September 2011 (Stats SA, 2011b) but does not announce its value. The Treasury website[80] offers no further enlightenment. The first LCS report holds out the promise of more to come – on p.3 it says that:

"… three additional products will be produced by Stats SA using the information gathered from the LCS 2008/2009, namely:

• Poverty Profile and Living Circumstances of the Poor
• Subjective and Relative Poverty in South Africa
• Men, Women and Children"

At the time of writing (June 2012) none of the promised reports had appeared. The necessary analysis must long since have been completed – the non-appearance of the results is a mystery. It has been rumoured that they were so awful that political pressure has been exerted to keep them under wraps – one sincerely hopes that this is not true.

Until government bestirs itself to make an announcement of what it thinks the poverty lines should be, we could do worse than make use of the poverty estimates prepared by Leibbrandt et al (2010).[81] From a menu of poverty lines (p.17) these

---

[80] http://www.treasury.gov.za/publications/other/povertyline/default.aspx), accessed 12 December 2011.

[81] Their major findings are that: "South Africa's high aggregate level of income inequality increased between 1993 and 2008. The same is true of inequality within each of South Africa's four major racial groups. Income poverty has fallen slightly in the aggregate but it persists at acute levels for the African and Coloured racial groups. Poverty in urban areas has increased. There have been continual improvements in non-monetary well-being (for example, access to piped water, electricity and formal housing) over the entire post-Apartheid period up to 2008." While the last of these offers some support to the Alkire et al MPI estimates, it will be shown below that important though these improvements have been, when it comes to broader measures of deprivation, they are outweighed by the parlous state of education and health services. As a matter of interest, if one is prepared to place any

authors select a pair they name South African Upper and Lower to demarcate what one of the authors has previously described as a 'poverty critical range'. The Upper line has a value of R949 and the Lower, R515 per capita per month in 2008 prices. Other than to say "Source: Own calculations on 2008 National Income Dynamics Survey", the box in the Leibbrandt *et al* paper (2010, p.17) does not disclose the origins of the R515 and R949 poverty lines. The R515 line is a bit higher than the Hoogeveen and Özler R322 per capita per month in 2000 prices – expressed in 2008 prices, R322 would be about R478.[82]

To soften the memory of the crass figures on South Africa presented in Table 1, let us cast a glance at some of the poverty estimates the lower of these two lines generates. Eyeballing the cumulative distribution functions (CDFs) in Figure 2.8 in their paper (p.42), for the year 2008 one sees that:

- Roughly 64 per cent of Africans, who make up almost four-fifths of the total population,[83] had incomes below the poverty line
- About 35 per cent of Africans had incomes less than half of the value of the poverty line.
- The bottom 20 per cent of Africans (about 16 per cent of the total population) had monthly incomes of roughly R150 per capita, less than one-third of the value of the poverty line.

Although a significant proportion of the households in which these folk live contain no children, or consist of a single adult, child poverty is still high, the Child Support Grant notwithstanding. In 2008:

- About 79 per cent of households contained one or more children
- Among these households the poverty headcount ratio (p_0) was 62 per cent

---

faith in subjective reports of well-being, Posel (2012, p.4), using data from the two waves of the National Income Dynamics Survey (NIDS), finds that not only are modal levels of life satisfaction much lower among the African population than among whites; but also that it fell for both groups between 2008 and 2010. Among Africans, out of a possible level of satisfaction of 10, 42 per cent reported a value of 4 or less in 2008. By 2010, that proportion had risen to 55 per cent. It would be crass to attempt to reduce this to tortoise-like progress in the struggle against poverty, and resentment against rising inequality, but they are in there, somewhere.

[82] The Hoogeveen and Özler food poverty line (R211 in 2000 prices) would have a value of about R313 in 2008 prices. The ratio of the Hoogeveen and Özler lower bound poverty line to the food line is about 1.52:1.00, whereas the corresponding ratio for the Leibbrandt *et al* lines is about 1.61:1.00.

[83] The proportion of Africans among the total population of 48.7 million in 2008 was 79.2 per cent. See Statistical release P0302, 30 July 2008, p.3.

- Their share of the poverty headcount was 91 per cent (Table 2.14, p.38)

Poverty among children was higher than in the population as a whole:

- In 2008, 23 per cent of the total population was in the age cohort 0-10 years
- The poverty headcount ratio among them was 67 per cent
- Their share of the poverty burden was 29 per cent (Table 2.15, p.38)

Poverty by education level of household head is revealing:

- Among all household heads, 18 per cent had no schooling
- The poverty headcount ratio among them was 80 per cent
- Their household's share of the total poverty burden was 27 per cent[84]

- Household heads with education levels between Grade1 and Grade 6 accounted for 20 per cent of the total
- The poverty headcount ratio among them was 76 per cent
- Their household's share of the total poverty burden was 28 per cent (Table 2.13, p.37)

Whatever one may say about the R515 poverty line, at least it does not suffer from the extreme sensitivity reported by Fischer (2010, p.37), where small changes in the value of the poverty line produced massive changes in poverty headcount ratios. The usual cause of heightened sensitivity of that sort is clustering of the poor in the region of the poverty line.

In South Africa, Africans account for 93 per cent of the poverty headcount, 94 per cent of the poverty gap, and the poverty headcount ratio among them was 0.64 (Leibbrandt et al, 2010, Table A3.11, p.82). Turning to the Leibbrandt et al cumulative distribution function for Africans for the year 2008 (2010, p.42) once more, and scaling off results around the poverty line, we see that if that line were allowed to fall by R55 to R470 (a 10.5 per cent decrease), it looks as though the headcount ratio would fall to 0.60 (a six per cent fall). Raising the poverty line by the same amount (to R580) would lead to a rise in the ratio to about 0.67 (a five per cent increase). So, among roughly 25 million poor Africans, if the poverty line were extended to R580, then within the range R470-580, there would be about 2.7 million people. Clustering of the poor around the poverty line is clearly not a problem in the Leibbrandt et al findings. In short, until such time as an authoritative set of

---

[84] The good news, partly caused by the decline in the proportion of household heads with zero education, and the rapid growth in the number of Child Support Grants disbursed, is that their share in 1993 had been 38 per cent (Leibbrandt et al, 2010, Table 2.13, p.37).

income/expenditure poverty estimates is produced and published, researchers (and government), the Leibbrandt *et al* figures are the best available.

If that view is accepted, then a careful look at both the World Bank poverty lines ($1.25/day etc) and the MDGs is necessary.[85] The *MDG Country Report 2010* (Stats SA, 2011a) notes that while South Africa is classified as a middle-income country, and as such faced an MDG poverty measure set at $2.50 a day, the "majority of the population qualifies the country as a low-income country... " This, according to Statistics South Africa is the "...sector where MDG 1 [eradicate extreme poverty and hunger] is applicable... " (p.23). The extreme poverty part of the goal having originally been expressed as halving the proportion of people living on less than $1 a day by the year 2015, that goal is now declared to have been achieved, while achievement of the revised measure of halving poverty at the $1.25/day line is said to be 'likely'. Not only that, the Country Report offers the opinion that halving poverty at the $2/day line is 'possible' (Stats SA, 2011a, p.24). To their credit, though, they do make the following caveat:

> "Although the target is achieved in terms of the MDGs targets as provided for at a $ 1 and $ 1.25 per day measure, poverty remains a reality in South Africa ..." (Stats SA, 2011a, p.29)

To put the 'achievements' in perspective, immediately after the caveat above, the MDG Report presents a set of figures for the year 2006 that allow us to form some idea of how much needs to be done before the 2015 MDG deadline is reached. These are presented in Table 4 below. The information provided by Stats SA is bolstered by estimates of the poverty headcounts at various World Bank ($/day) poverty lines, and by estimates of the rand value of average incomes in each category. The story is not a happy one. Forget about PPPs for a moment and read through the list below of the retail prices (in 2006 prices) of some of the items consumed by poor people in October-December 2006. In that period, the average cost of a 700 gram loaf of white bread was R4.78; brown bread was R4.35. A 420 gram can of baked beans cost R3.83; potatoes were about R2.00/kg; French Polony (compressed meat scraps, offal and probably Red Dye No. 2) a staple food of very poor people, cost R16.61/kg; a whole fresh chicken was R21.80; one litre of fresh low fat milk cost R4.77; half-a-dozen eggs cost about R5.90; a 425 gram can of

---

[85] The paper by Fischer (2010) cited earlier is highly critical of the MDGs, noting that on the one hand that: "It is very difficult to know the impact of the MDGs on poverty reduction [because] poverty measurements are ambiguous, arbitrary and contested" while on the other: "the mechanisms by which MDGs might have effected poverty reduction are not at all clear... " (p.36)

pilchards in tomato sauce (another staple for poor people) cost R7.60, while sugar was about R5.50/kg (NAMC, 2006, pp.17-26).

Table 4 Poverty nine years before the 2015 halving deadline

Poverty line		Poverty	Headcount	Average income	
(PPP$/day)	(R/day)	ratio (%)	(millions)	$/day	R/day
1.00	3.50	5.0	2.4	0.77	2.70
1.25	4.43	9.7	4.6	0.95	3.33
2.00	6.93	25.3	12.0	1.36	4.76
2.50	8.97	34.8	16.5	1.60	5.60
Source: Stats SA, 2011a, p.29 and own calculations. Note: 2006 population (47.4 million) figure used to estimate headcounts is from Statistics release P0302, 16 August 2006, p.1.					

At the very lowest line, $1.00/day, there were 2.4 million people whose average income (one assumes it is higher than the median income of those below the line) of $0.77/day, translates into R2.70/day (in 2006 prices). This would have been sufficient to buy half-a-loaf of white bread, and maybe 100 grams of French Polony. Those at the upper bound of this category may have been able to buy half-a-loaf of bread, and a third share in a can of pilchards. All told, there were almost ten million people living on less than R4.43/day.

Readers are invited to dip into *The South African Food Cost Review: 2006* (NAMC, 2006) to glimpse the array of choices that opens up when one reaches such dizzying heights as the $2.00/day level (approximately R7/day).[86] My sense of it is that for those sharing the pot with a few others of roughly equal income, starvation may be averted. There will, however, be precious little left over to buy anything else.

If the food poverty line has been set at R209 per capita per month in 2006 prices by Statistics South Africa, then they appear not to have erred on the side of generosity. This could mean that a domestic poverty line, if one ever appears, could be well below that proposed by Leibbrandt *et al*. This, in turn, could make poverty look less bad.

It should hardly be necessary to remind anyone of the intensely political nature of debates about poverty. What the lines considered above tell us (if anything) about

---

[86] Those of creative bent may care to write a guide to 'Feeding a family of four on R12/day', like Mrs Beeton did for the respectable poor in Victorian England.

people's conditions of existence, therefore, matters a great deal. Politicians, especially when under siege by poor people clamouring for relief, for jobs, for food, are likely to grasp at any straw offered by researchers. So although it may be argued that halving the headcount ratio at any poverty line is to be celebrated, that celebration must needs be muted if its basis is as parsimonious as the World Bank poverty lines on display above.

Equally importantly, if population growth causes the headcount to increase or remain constant, rather than fall over the period under consideration, not even one cheer would be in order. Celebration of the 'hope that halving poverty at the $2/day level is possible', if that level is roughly equal to the food poverty line, and if the headcount at that level does not fall, would clearly be inappropriate. Yet it is not inconceivable that the political elite could ignore Statistics South Africa's caveat about 'poverty remaining a reality in South Africa', and go ahead and celebrate it anyway.

With that, we turn to South Africa's education system.

Section 4 South Africa's dysfunctional education system

Apartheid's legacy in the form of its education policy is still clearly visible almost two decades after the accession to power of the first democratic government in 1994. As is well known, apartheid offered relatively high quality education to whites, less generous provision for 'Indians/Asiatics', less again for the population mainly of 'mixed' blood (so-called coloureds), and what is popularly described as 'bantustan' education for the (black) African population.[87] The latter system, designed to keep people in a state of servitude, exploded in revolt in 1976 (the Soweto riots), arguably the event that announced the beginning of the end of apartheid.

Despite major achievements since 1994, such as the unification of 19 separate departments of education into a single national department; the design of (some) good policy, and the creation of an impressive legislative structure, commentators are united in their view that all of this effort has done little to improve the quality of education that is the lot of the majority of schoolchildren. Although enrolment rates have risen[88] and there are now millions more attending school, the consensus is that somewhere in the region of 80 per cent of schools are dysfunctional. The numbers of science and mathematics passes among black African pupils in the final year of high school is pathetically small, in both absolute and relative terms. On the international stage, the performance, on average, of South African schoolchildren is abysmal, and not much better when compared with their counterparts elsewhere in Africa.

Under normal circumstances, it would be unusual to find one government department exposing or acknowledging the dismal performance of other departments. Circumstances in South Africa are, however, far from what are almost taken for granted in developed countries (several of which also have serious problems in health and education). In 2009, a National Planning Commission, charged with "developing a draft long term vision and strategic plan for South Africa", was created in the Presidency. In November 2011, the Commission (many

---

[87] The use of racial classifications reminiscent of the apartheid era is the subject of vigorous debate in South Africa (and elsewhere). Because official statistics in South Africa are still collected using these categories, those who make use of them are obliged to take a stand on how to proceed. In the present paper I stick to the liberal convention of describing the four population groups as African (occasionally with the descriptor 'black'), Indian/Asian, coloured (mainly mixed origin) and white. Analytically, these categories are slowly losing some of their significance. Appropriately or not, however, many issues are still cast in racial terms.

[88] In 2009, "Participation in education programmes amongst 7-to-15 year olds" stood at 98.5 per cent, up from 96.3 per cent in 2002. See Department of Basic Education, 2011, p.25. See also the MDG Country Report (Stats SA, 2011a, p.49).

of whose members were drawn from civil society) published the *National Development Plan*, subtitled *Vision for 2030* (NPC, 2011). Two critiques – one on the education sector, the other on health – in an Appendix at the end of the present paper, have been extracted from the Plan.

Although the original cause of the problems in education is the set of obstacles left behind by apartheid, the bad performance of the sector since the advent of democracy in 1994 lies elsewhere. The Commission's view on this matter (which is not to say that it is necessarily correct) is that:

"Two factors are largely responsible for the failings of the school system. The primary cause is weak capacity throughout the civil service – teachers, principals and system-level officials, which results not only in poor schooling outcomes, but also breeds a lack of respect for government. The mirror image of this weakness in the technical core is a culture of patronage that permeates almost all areas of the civil service. Nepotism and the appointment of unsuitable personnel further weaken government capacity." (NPC, 2011, pp.269-270).

Into this mess marched Alkire and Santos, armed with the two indicators reported above, namely:

- Years of Schooling – If no household member has completed 5 years schooling
- Child school attendance – If any school-aged child is out of school in years 1-8

Given national participation rates for 7-15 year olds in excess of 98 per cent in 2009, one would not expect the second of these indicators to trouble the scorers greatly (which is not to deny that performance in some provinces in this regard, is not all it should be). Of far greater importance, however, are the limitations of the latter indicator, to which they themselves draw attention.

"… school attendance", they note, "does not capture completion, quality of schooling, or skills. But it is the best indicator possible to indicate whether or not school-aged children are being exposed to a learning environment." (Alkire and Santos, 2010a, p.14)

These drawbacks, especially the absence of information on quality,[89] are precisely those that would reveal the fact that a substantial proportion of the South Africa's population faces the risk of lifetime exclusion from participation in a rapidly-changing cultural milieu, one of whose entry tickets are literacy and numeracy.

The first of their selected indicators is interesting. Their justification for its use builds on the idea of "*effective* literacy" (their emphasis) which suggests that:

> "… all household members benefit from the abilities of a literate person in the household, regardless of each person's actual level of education." (Alkire and Santos, 2010a, p.14)

Two rather obvious questions about this indicator present themselves: the first of them asks if it can be taken for granted that someone who has completed five years of schooling is literate? The second wants to know how reliable an indicator the presence is of such a person, of the existence of a 'learning environment'? Whether or not one can reasonably claim that having someone in the household with five years of education, shows that the household is not educationally deprived, is moot. This is because 'years of education' is not a good proxy for literacy. Figure 3 below, is reproduced from a major study by van der Berg *et al* in the University of Stellenbosch (2011, p.7), casts a spotlight on *Low Quality Education as a poverty trap*. The results illustrate in fairly stark fashion what can happen to analyses if education quality is ignored.

Published literacy scores are often crude assumptions based on years of education.[90] The results in Figure 3, by contrast, come from the 2007 survey conducted for the Southern and East African Consortium for Monitoring Educational Quality (SAQMEC), a survey specially designed to measure mathematical and reading skills (Spaull, 2011). For those lucky enough to be in historically white schools, maximum density (modal value) of literacy scores of those in grade 5 occurs in the region of about 80 per cent. In the historically black schools the corresponding figure looks as though it is about 35 per cent, roughly half the literacy score at maximum density for those in grade 3 in the historically white schools.[91] Most of the grade 3 pupils in historically white schools (now much more racially integrated)

---

[89] The fact that the WHS does not (cannot?) provide Alkire and Santos with any data on school attendance (Alkire and Santos, 2010a, p26n) should not be allowed to distract attention away from the importance of acquiring information on education quality.

[90] One of the definitions used by Statistics South Africa classifies those beyond school-going age as functionally illiterate if their highest level of education is lower than Grade 7. See the General Household Survey for 2009 – Statistical release P0318, 6 May 2010, p.4.

[91] For an analysis of the persistence of educational under-achievement over successive generations, see Burns and Keswell, 2011.

had higher literacy scores than the grade 5 pupils in historically black schools (attended almost exclusively by black African kids).[92] Not only do these distributions (which are bimodal for the sample as a whole) illustrate how serious the problem of illiteracy is, they also show the effect that generations of poverty, inequality and low quality education can have.

Figure 3 Literacy scores in historically black schools and white schools (2007)

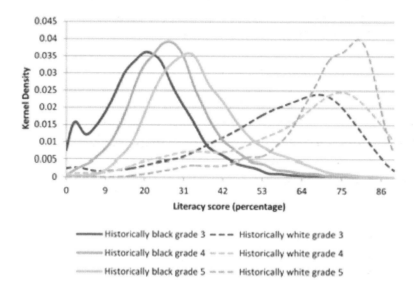

Source: van der Berg *et al*, 2011, p.7.

In 2008, the Department of Basic Education introduced an in-house test (presumably similar to the SAQMEC) in literacy/language and numeracy/mathematics. The 2009 results for grade 3 pupils produced average aggregates in literacy and numeracy of 39 and 44 per cent respectively (50 per cent was deemed a pass). Pass rates were 33 and 41 per cent respectively for the two assessments. Performances of the grade 6 pupils were worse – a mere 13 per cent of pupils passed mathematics, while 20 per cent passed language. Average aggregates were 30 and 31 per cent (Department of Basic Education, 2011, p.47). The report from which this information comes, says nothing about the tests being conducted in historically black schools only. If the figures are nationally representative, the performance of pupils from historically black schools will be even worse than those given above.

---

[92] See Shepherd, 2011, p.9.

As far as the benefits of the presence of an 'educated' individual in the household are concerned, it is certainly true that many poor people believe firmly in the emancipatory power of education, a commitment evidenced by the "extraordinary sacrifices" they are prepared to make to propel a child, or grandchild through school (Fleisch, 2008, p.77).[93] In the passage immediately preceding this comment, however, Fleisch observes that:

> "There are a number of studies now available, both quantitative and qualitative, that show the ways in which poor families transmit restricted language and literary practices to their children. In the absence of school-aligned practices taught at home, poor children are at a decided disadvantage as they enter the school gates to learn to read and do mathematics. The limited vocabulary and restricted experience with books and printed texts means that they have to catch up from the start."

While this is undoubtedly true, there is also evidence to suggest that children from low 'socio-economic status' (SES) households who are fortunate enough to escape into high SES schools, experience gains from schooling similar to those of children from wealthier backgrounds. The likely explanation for this in the South African case is said to be the:

> "… better school management, greater parental and governing body involvement, sufficient school discipline, little teacher absenteeism, high teacher quality and motivation, and generally a more functional school environment… " (Spaull, 2011, p.18)[94]

These are the variables that perforce are disregarded when quality of schooling cannot be taken into account – precisely the variables on which poor, failing schools score badly.

The link between poverty and poor performance can be made visible in numerous ways. Instead of presenting school results by racial classification, Shepherd (2011, p.32) plots reading tests scores as measured by the 2006 *Progress in International Reading Literacy Study* (PIRLS) against socio-economic status (SES). Figure 4 below, reproduced from Figure 3 in the Shepherd paper, shows quite clearly that low

---

[93] The same must be true, even for, or maybe especially for many illiterate people.

[94] For a view that stresses the continuing salience of race, even for black kids who have attended some of South Africa's top schools, see the two-part article by Max Price, Vice-Chancellor of the University of Cape Town in the *Mail & Guardian*. The first part, "In defence of race-based policy", was in the January 6, 2012 edition of the paper, while the second, "Past sins revisited and corrected", appeared a week later on January 13, 2012.

SES pupils perform less well in both the 'African' and 'English/Afrikaans' schools. The difference between peak performance in the latter is, however, appears to be much greater in the latter than the former. It is likely that many of the low SES pupils are Black (African), thus calling into question, the findings by Spaull reported above. Although for certain purposes, race may be of some interest, it is socio-economic status that is of importance here.

Figure 4 Reading test score distribution by school type, and student SES

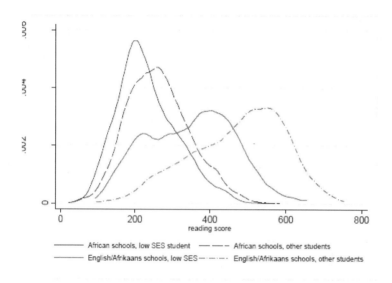

Source: Shepherd, 2011, p.32.

Between 'other students' in the 'English/Afrikaans' schools and 'low SES' students in African schools, differences in peak performance (maximum kernel density) are enormous – a reading score of about 200 for the latter vs. 550 or so for the former.

Another way in which the link between poverty and poor performance is demonstrated may be found in the pages of *Mathematics and Science Achievement at South African Schools in TIMMS 2003* [Trends in International Mathematics and Science Studies]. This source of evidence of the poor performance of all except a handful of schoolchildren, Reddy *et al* (2006, p.46) plots mathematics scores against HDIs by province.[95] Top of the chart is the Western Cape, the province with the

---

[95] As noted earlier, provincial HDIs come originally from the National HDR for South Africa (UNDP, 2003). Different rankings of poverty and deprivation are produced by different measures, with some swopping of rank in the middle of the distribution. One thing

lowest incidence of poverty, while at the bottom are to be found the provinces with the largest concentrations of black African populations, many stuck in poor rural areas (Limpopo, Eastern Cape, North West Province, KwaZulu-Natal and Mpumalanga). Incidentally, the Western Cape score of 389 was well below the international average of 467, and light years away from the Singapore average score of 605 (Mullis *et al*, 2004, p.34). At the 95th percentile, the score was about 480, a little over the international average. The South African national average of 264 was the lowest recorded score among the countries that took part in the test.

Delving into the root causes of poor performance that are not attributable to systemic incompetence, the authors of the National Development Plan (NPC, 2011) commence their analysis of the challenges in education with an examination of the nutritional status of pre-school children. It may be recalled that as the second indicator for the health dimension of the MPI, Alkire and Santos use "Nutrition – If any adult or child in the family is malnourished". In South Africa, the Commission claims that:

"There are 2.8 million households and 11.5 million individuals who are vulnerable to hunger, over 72 percent of whom live in rural areas." (NPC, 2011, p.269)

This is followed by an account of dietary insufficiencies that suggests malnourishment on a grand scale. On the issue of micronutrients deficiencies, Fleisch comments that:

"Along with long-term psychological effects of low protein energy diets, insufficient micronutrients in the diet is (*sic*) estimated to affect half of all South African schoolchildren and is likely to have an equally dramatic impact on learning. While it is known that food insufficiency is a serious problem affecting children's ability to learn, evidence has shown that a deficiency in micronutrients such as iron deficiency can result in slower child development in the domains of language learning and motor skills. The problem is that iron deficiency develops slowly in children and seldom produces acute symptoms, though as the problem becomes worse, children do become pale and weak, eat less and tire easily. These children are more susceptible to respiratory illnesses and intestinal infections." (2008, p.35)[96]

---

that does not vary is the placing of the Western Cape at the top of the pile, and the competition between the Eastern Cape and Limpopo for the bottom position. See Table 6 in Basirir, 2011, p.484.

[96] Alkire and Santos (2010a) are well aware of the effects of malnutrition and micro-nutrient deficiency (as one would expect them to be). See, for example, the discussion on p.10.

In their haste to stress the need for measures of multi-dimensional deprivation, some the evangelists tend to be a trifle cavalier about income poverty. There is also a tendency, when proselytizing, to behave as though those given to the estimation of uni-dimensional poverty measures were unaware that poverty is multi-dimensional. Income poverty is serious – anyone who has gone hungry, if only for a couple of days, knows that when one does not have the wherewithal with which to feed oneself, thoughts of how to exercise one's other capabilities, fade somewhat in significance. Yet Alkire and Santos were somehow able to make it seem as though the 20-25 per cent of the South African population whose incomes or expenditure levels have been shown above to lie below the food poverty line, did not suffer multiple deprivation. The very idea that educational deprivation among children in these households could have been as low as Alkire and Santos suggested was preposterous – the 'lower bound' fig leaf served merely to provide skimpy cover for what looked more and more like an embarrassing mistake, as it was disclosed in the fullness of time to be.

We could carry on like this for ages – if, for some reason, confronting a dismal set of income poverty estimates fails to impress, or if neither Fleisch nor the National Planning Commission are held to be sufficiently informative or authoritative, one could dip into the work of others. Graeme Bloch's *The Toxic Mix: What's wrong with South Africa's schools and how to fix it* (2009) would be a good place to start. In it, he pays tribute to the OECD's *Reviews of National Policies for Education – South Africa* (2008), which draws similarly dismal conclusions to his own (albeit in more restrained terms). Under-qualified primary school teachers, many unable to pass standard tests, are but one of the many failures to which attention is drawn. On the other side of barriers, Zwelinzima Vavi, secretary-general of the Congress of South African Trade Unions (Cosatu), the country's largest trade union federation, and ANC alliance partner, thunders against the inequity and inefficiency and the "catastrophe" of an education system that consigns the children of working-class parents to a "deep black hole". After discussing high dropout and failure rates, and the inescapable contrast between the good performance in former 'white' schools and the inferior education and infrastructure in that part of the system that caters to the poor, he turned to the vexed topic of teachers. The "system", he said, "had also "demoralized" teachers, with 55% saying they would leave the profession if given the opportunity… "[97] He was also balanced enough in his approach to call for:

---

[97] The 55 per cent disgruntled is cited in the *OECD Review* (2008, p.23). The *Review*, while less overtly critical than other work cited here, offers a fine and detailed (if a little dated) account of the education system in South Africa.

"… a "change of mind-set" in teachers as well as the adoption of zero-tolerance towards teachers who arrived late for work or left early."[98]

It is fitting that we end this peep into the broad, if somewhat depressing landscape of education in South Africa with a hint at future struggles. Teachers, who for a while were renamed 'educators' (in the same spirit, presumably as that which caused pupils to be re-imagined as learners), are at the centre of those struggles. From his analysis of South Africa's education crisis, Bloch concludes that:

"Getting teachers right is priority number one if schools are going to work. It will require a mixture of support and laying down the line,[99] an acknowledgement of the complexity of teaching and the many difficulties faced by teachers, alongside a set of demands laying out exactly what is expected of the teachers in our classrooms." (Bloch, 2009, p.22)

It were surprising if the authors of *Vision for 2030* (NPC, 2011) had not arrived at the same conclusion – in exchange for extensive training and upgrading of skills, and the reduction of bureaucratic incompetence and other factors that cause teachers to waste precious hours each schoolday,[100] they will be required to submit themselves to tests of competency – those who fail will be "removed through formal procedures". Strikes, which in the past have descended into violence, in future:

"… must occur within the law. Criminal behavior will be prosecuted, and teacher indiscipline will be punished. There will be no "political solutions" to incidents of lawlessness and indiscipline." (NPC, 2011, p.281)

A policy prescription of this sort was bound to stir up controversy – the fun and games started almost immedaitely – on 2 December 2011, Basic Education Minister

---

[98] See the article by Karl Gernetzky "Poor schools a deep, black hole – Vavi" in *Business Day*, 29 September 2011.
[99] Not for nothing has the slogan 'in class, on time, teaching' been adopted by all committed to the improvement of education in South Africa. The slogan emerged as part of a resolution taken at the Polokwane congress of the ANC in 2009 following which President Mbeki was deposed (redeployed) and President Zuma was installed in his place. See Bloch, 2009, p.20. It is possible, however, to ladle too much of the blame for the failures of the education system onto incompetent and/or unmotivated teachers. Scapegoating might be a comfort to some, but simplistic analyses with their superficial policy prescriptions do not contribute much. For a nuanced discussion of the issue of teacher competence (and schooling in general), see the paper by van der Berg *et al*, 2011, p.5. See also the paper by Shepherd (2011) on 'what prevents poor schools from delivering results'.
[100] Bloch reports that "[t]eachers in township schools spend 3.5 hours per day on instruction, compared to 6 hours per day in suburban schools." (DBSA, 2008, p.31)

Angie Motshega "… slammed Planning Minister Trevor Manuel's National Development Plan, calling it unrealistic". Although she was talking about "performance-based pay", she quickly found "… an unlikely ally in the SA Democratic Teachers' Union", which "… said testing teachers would be an "insult" and would worsen their "low morale".[101]

If the plans that the Department of Basic Education has for the future[102] come to fruition, improvements should slowly be made – possibly a decade or so of

---

[101] See the article "Trevor's plan 'unrealistic': Angie" by Retha Grobbelaar in *Times Live*, 2 December 2011. Objections raised by the Minister and the teacher's union attracted immediate criticism from Wilmot James, shadow Minister of Basic Education in the official opposition party, the DA (Democratic Alliance). He is reported as saying that: "Their resistance to the NDP's call for competency tests for teachers, performance-based pay and the non-interference of unions in the appointment and promotion of teachers and officials constitutes an unprincipled obstruction to achieving educational excellence for South African schools." Downloaded from http://www.politicsweb.co.za/politicsweb/view/politicsweb/en/page71619?oid=270048&sn=Marketingweb+detail, accessed 5 December 2011.
For an update on the continuing fight by national government to regain control of the finances in provinces racking up billions in overspending, see the accounts of attempts by the Department of Basic Education to stamp its authority on the Eastern Cape in the *Mail & Guardian* ("Intervention needed in EC education department", by Bongani Nkosi, 17 February 2012), and *Business Day* ("Motshekga to get tougher on Eastern Cape", Carol Paton, 20 February 2012).
[102] See, for example the *Action Plan to 2014*, Department of Basic Education, 2010. There is a long way to go – some of the provincial education departments are so incompetent and corrupt that they are not even capable of ensuring that schoolchildren have available to them, the books necessary to begin each new year. By June this year (2012) schools in the Limpopo province had not received books that were supposed to have been distributed in January. Not even a court order could unblock the bureaucracy. So serious is the problem that unusually for government, the Department of Basic Education commissioned jointly with an NGO, Section 27, an inquiry into what had gone wrong (Metcalfe, 2012). The report makes distressing reading – the causes of the disaster (for schoolkids deprived of books for half of an academic year) are deep and systemic. The press has had a field day, and the scandal has yet to die down. See, for example, the article "Great concern' as government still fails to deliver Limpopo textbooks: Minister to apologise after Department of Basic Education misses court-ordered deadline to deliver textbooks to all schools in Limpopo" by Karl Gernetzky in *Business Day*, 20 June 2012. A few days after that article appeared, the story acquired the strong whiff of corruption, causing the official opposition to demand an inquiry into the Minister's involvement in the awarding of the tender for book delivery to a firm with a history of fraud and incompetence. See *Mail & Guardian*, 24 June 2012, "DA: Probe Motshekga, EduSolutions relationship". With each passing day, the scandal deepens. The company responsible for failing to deliver books on time, EDuSolutions, a major contributor to the ANC, is revealed as being connected to the

incremental change will usher in a new era. Mass poverty, however, constitutes a significant barrier. As was shown above, some 40-50 per cent of South Africa's population is believed to be in poverty (depending on how one measures it) – at the bottom end of this group, about 20 per cent of the population is chronically poor. Half of all schoolchildren are said to be malnourished. Not all of them will be located in poor households, but it is certain that the vast majority of them will be. Should mass poverty persist (and it shows little sign of being reduced, let alone eradicated), it will continue to act as a drag on the best-laid plans. The crisis in education will rumble on, and 'learners' will be chained by low capability to their poverty. Even optimistic commentators like the authors of the country report for 2010 on the MDGs (Stats SA, 2011a)[103] acknowledge that:

"… what remains worrisome is the quality of education and in particular the quantitative faculties and literacy as well. Furthermore major socio-economic obstacles continue, however, to retard progress on the provision of quality education." (2011, p.49).

The conclusion that I drew in Versions 1 and 2 of the paper was that unless the Alkire and Santos MPI for South Africa was reconstructed using appropriate indicators, attempts to 'isolate the reality' of crises like those which beset the country's education system must fail. Reliant as it was on a relatively small, albeit well-designed survey, and constrained, because of the international scope of the project, by a limited menu of variables from which to choose, the MPI for South Africa presented in the 2010 *Human Development Report* never had a hope of

---

President. See the article "Textbook boss's links to Zuma" by Sally Evans in the *Mail & Guardian*, 6 July 2012. An editorial in the paper on the same day probed into the 'Thunder, smoke and mirrors' emanating from government's vain attempt to disguise the seriousness of the situation. See also "SIU probes senior officials in textbook shame" by Jonathan Erasmus on the same day. In another article, denial of corruption and incompetence in the procurement process by the Minister for Basic Education is shown to be without any basis – apart from the fuss made by activists and NGOs at the end of the previous school year, a scathing police report on tender-related abuse requested in March 2012, was delivered a month later. Earlier investigations (January 2011) by the *Mail & Guardian* newspaper had revealed corruption involving book sellers and distributors – see David McFarlane, "Denial an 'other force' to be reckoned with", 6 July 2012. An interesting confession by Cosatu (Congress of South African Trade Unions) general secretary Zwelinzima Vavi, in an article by Natasha Marrian in *Business Day* on 9 July 2012 under the heading "Textbook fiasco 'an own goal' for SA's leaders" acknowledges that it is because the elite is out of touch with the masses (and the union with its membership!) that such disasters can take place.
[103] The tone of the MDG country report for 2010 is generally upbeat and uncritical, discovering, for example, literacy rates among 15-24 year-olds in 2009 of 89 and 93 per cent for females and males respectively (Stats SA, 2011a, p.45). As pointed out above, the definition of literacy used is suspect.

saying anything useful about a socio-economic problem, the like of which has been sketched above.

That conclusion still stands. Despite switching to a survey that gives more plausible results, the indicators chosen to discover the extent of educational deprivation cannot do the job. Glance back at Figures 1 and 2 at the start of the paper – education's contribution to the MPI is now about seven per cent of the total. This is not plausible – if the brief account of the crisis in education given above is pointing in the correct direction, and if the weighting of the health and education dimensions remains equal, as Alkire and Santos have assumed it to be, then I suspect that education will be able to hold its own against health, as contributor to the deprivation of South Africa's poor.

Section 5 Health, AIDS, Tuberculosis, STIs and violent death

Renowned for its scenic beauty, its wildlife, its unique flora and its vibrant culture, South Africa is also well-known to rank among the most unequal societies on earth. Arrived at the gleaming new Cape Town International airport, the visitor is confronted, indeed, cannot avoid mile after mile of squatter housing as they make their way along a six-lane highway to the first-world amenities of the city. Were they to inquire into the state of affairs in health in South Africa, they would soon learn that (i) the country is in the grip of an AIDS epidemic;[104] (ii) access to quality health care is for the privileged few who can afford to pay the insurance premiums (this should surely come as no surprise), and that (iii) after many years of indifferent reform, the state has finally started to tackle the monumental task of improving the quality of health services delivered mainly to poor people.

Apropos the first of these, one would have thought that an essential quality of an index that claims to be 'policy relevant' is that it be capable, at least, of picking up (isolating) the changes in morbidity and mortality that an epidemic of this nature causes. The MPI, however, appears to be blissfully unaware of the event. Given this, before plunging into the two topics identified above, let us take a brief look at the indicators that Alkire and Santos selected for measuring the health dimension of the MPI. As the following passage reveals, doing so was no easy task for them:

> "… health was the most difficult dimension to measure. Comparable indicators of health for all household members are generally missing from household surveys. Yet the capability to live a long and healthy life is a basic capability and is also the prerequisite for much of human development." (2010a, p.14)

In other words, the imperative to include a health dimension in the MPI is strong, so strong that an attempt to stare down the difficulties simply has to be made. Admirable though this commitment may sound (a measure *will* be constructed, willy-nilly?), it makes no concession to the possibility that for some countries, a plausible set of health indicators cannot be constructed along the lines that they propose. The argument in this section is that at least in the South African case, the chosen indicators cannot possibly do the job. The indicators they use, it may be recalled, are the following:

---

[104] Not to mention tuberculosis and violence – Coovadia (2009, p.1) argues that "South Africa has four concurrent epidemics, a health …. Poverty-related illnesses … such as infectious diseases, maternal death, and malnutrition, remain widespread, and there is a growing burden of non-communicable diseases. HIV/AIDS accounts for 31% of the total disability-adjusted life years of the South African population, with violence and injuries constituting a further cause of premature deaths [6.5 per cent of the total] and disability."

- Child mortality – If any child has died in the family
- Nutrition – If any adult or child in the family is malnourished

With regard to the former of these, it is well known that mortality rates for children are not easy to measure. A recent article by McKerrow and Mulaudzi (2010) on the reliability of the South African estimates works its way through many of the problems encountered in trying to pin down this sad statistic. So severe are the difficulties that it does not appear to be possible to construct from competing estimates, a reliable time series (McKerrow and Mulaudzi, 2010, p.63). Another indication of the difficulties faced is visible in the acknowledgement by the Department of Health that the South African Demographic and Health Survey (SADHS) estimates of fertility and child mortality for the year 2003, are "implausibly low" and that there is no:

> "… obvious way in which these estimates could be reliably adjusted to allow for the data inadequacies in a consistent manner." (DoH, 2007, p.xix).

Among the 10 200 households targeted for inclusion in the survey, the response rate was 85 per cent (DoH, 2007, p.xix). Although it is impossible to say without detailed investigation (such as an examination of relative sampling errors), whether or not the WHS (the small survey that provided the data on the basis of which the estimate of the 2003 South African MPI were made) has more success than the DHS in measuring child and infant mortality, it is nonetheless useful to look at some of the features of the WHS.

Digging into the description of the WHS data, my first reaction was one of surprise at the small number of usable cases that had been dragged out of survey (a discovery that served to heighten my scepticism about the ability of the MPI to deliver on the 'policy relevance' front). Sample size was 3158 households. The response rate was 80 per cent (2528 households). In these households, 2576 individuals were selected for interview – 2319 were interviewed (WHO, 2003, p.13).[105] Details of "Item Non Response (mean per cent missing per section)" in various sections of the WHS are given in Table 2.3.4 in the WHS report for South Africa (WHO, 2003, p.14). In the Mortality section of the survey, non-response was about 18 per cent, while the mean percentage missing in the Demographics section looks to be almost 30 per cent.

---

[105] The WHS was instituted by the World Health Organization (WHO) in 2000/2001 as part of the Global Program on Evidence for Health Policy (GPE). GPE Paper No. 37 (Üstün et al, 2001) contains most of the information on the survey that the interested reader is likely to require. Sample size for the 2003 South African WHS handsomely exceeded that laid down as a minimum in the sampling guidelines (WHO, 2002a)

Mortality, always difficult to measure in a developing-country context, features high of the list of suspected causes of gross errors made in the 2003 MPI.

Depending on the variable under consideration, a survey of such modest size may well be able to provide some satisfactory information. When, however, it is child deaths that are at issue, the likelihood that anything sensible can be said diminishes sharply (witness the abrupt change in the proportional contributions of child deaths to the MPI disclosed in Figures 1 and 2 above).[106]

As far as the reliability of the WHS is concerned, a fair amount of information, obtained by estimating Kappa coefficients,[107] is available. The Nigerian WHS, among the least reliable of the surveys, had a response rate of 98 per cent; missing data amounted to 11.5 per cent, while the percentage of items for which Kappa was greater than 0.4 (fair agreement) amounted to no more than 45 per cent (Üstün et al, 2001, p.126). In some countries, the health component of the survey performs poorly. Table 8a in Üstün et al (p.39) shows that the Kappa values among seven 'health items' obtained from ten countries whose survey was conducted in the 'full-length Household Interview mode', averaged about 0.65 (good agreement), while the average at the bottom end of the range of values was 0.28 (fair agreement).

Table 2.3.5 in the WHS report for South Africa (WHO, 2003, p.15) gives Kappa values for a number of items. Unfortunately there are no explanatory notes, so that when one comes to look at the Kappa values for mortality, instead of a single value,

---

[106] If there were about 14 million households in South Africa in 2011, and 50 500 deaths of children aged under five in that year, then the crude probability of a death occurring in any household (a flow variable) would have been 0.0036. Among a sample of 2500 households (apart from bias caused by non-response), nine could thus expect a visit from the Angel of Death. Even though the probability story is more complicated than this, the needle-in-a-haystack nature of the search is clear. What makes matters worse, as Alkire and Santos themselves point out, is that the reliability of child mortality as an indicator in the WHS is further compromised by the nature of the available data. In their words: "This indicator is particularly problematic. It is a stock indicator, because the year of death of the child is not recorded in most surveys – so the death could have happened many years ago." Ever the optimists, though, they end the paragraph thus: "However given the absence of health functioning information on household members, it provides at least rudimentary information on health functionings." (2010a, p15)

[107] They measure the 'agreement' between responses in the original survey, and those obtained from retests conducted on a sample of the original respondents. The values generally range between zero and a maximum of unity (implying perfect agreement). Negative values are possible but relatively rare. A Kappa value <0.2 betokens poor agreement; 0.20-0.4, fair agreement; 0.4-0.6, moderate agreement; 0.6-0.8, good agreement, and 0.8-1.0, very good agreement. The South African WHS retested 154 respondents (WHO, 2003, p.15).

one finds that there are three (they range from just below zero to a high of about 0.47, with an intermediate value of about 0.4 (fair agreement), leaving one at somewhat of a loss to understand what they mean. As we have seen above, the missing data results are less equivocal.

There is not much information on reliability in the Alkire and Santos 2010a paper – what is given is, however, is quite revealing. Appendix 2 in the paper gives sample sizes and non-response rates. Table 2.1 (p.116) in the appendix tells us that total sample size for the South African WHS was 10 633 (among whom, as we have noted above, 2319 were interviewed). The weighted percentage of the total sample used to compute the MPI was 57.93 (the unweighted percentage was 57.39) – which suggests that usable results were obtained from about 1330 cases. Reductions in sample sizes", they inform us, "were due to missing data". These are detailed by indicator in Table 2.2 (p.120). Without explanatory notes, some of them are more than a trifle misleading. Unweighted non-response for schooling was a plausible 0.38 per cent, while that for mortality was a round 0.00. This would make sense only if the non-response rates were estimated after the sample had been reduced because of missing data (unusable case had been removed).

It is not unreasonable to expect bias to be introduced following the drastic reductions caused by missing values. Readers may recall that it is missing values that form the basis of their 'lower bound' caveat). The reason why Alkire and Santos arrived at the decision to attach that label to the results for South Africa (and a few other countries), may be found in the discussion of the way they tested for bias[108] – here is the description of the procedure adopted to deal with missing values on the basis of which they concluded that the MPI estimates for certain countries were to be treated as 'lower bound estimates':[109]

> "… some countries have important sample reductions due to missing values in one or more variables (*typically nutrition*). For those countries we have compared the percent of deprived population in each of the other indicators in the group with missing values in the indicator under analysis with that of the group with observed values in the indicator under analysis, performing hypothesis tests of difference in means." (2010a, p.29, emphasis added)

Malnutrition, as it affects education, was glanced at in the previous section of the paper. The Alkire and Santos 2010a paper performs cluster analysis of the ten

---

[108] Discussion of the treatment of the non-applicable population and of missing values may be found on pp.26ff of the Alkire and Santos (2010a) paper.
[109] The warning about estimates being lower bounds only is repeated on p.80 in Table 1.1 of their paper.

indicators that go to make up the MPI, using the approach to develop a typology of different forms of poverty (pp.51-53). Values of individual indicators are given for a few countries, and poverty types for many more. Unfortunately, South Africa does not appear to be among them. A search, admittedly cursory, failed to disclose any malnutrition figures for South Africa derived from the WHS. Without digging into the survey itself (or writing to the authors) it is not known what the MPI malnutrition score was. On this question, the South African literature seems united in its gloominess – the chapter on nutrition by Swart *et al* in the *2008 South African Health Review* concluded that the nutritional status of South Africans did not improve between the democratic elections of 1994 and 2005.[110]

So much for the reliability of the Alkire and Santos health indicators. In the face of this impasse, the sensible thing to do is to leave the question of the reliability of the MPI hanging, and turn instead, to a subject on which the WHS may have the potential to say interesting things, namely, the health of the health system.

A tale of two health care systems

As with the education system in South Africa, so it is with the health system – much of it is dysfunctional. Like the education sector, which has several fine private schools in South Africa catering to a tiny (rich) minority, and many independent schools catering to non-rich parents anxious to avoid the national school system, the private sector health care system caters for a substantial minority (the well-off and formal-economy workers), in what private sector commentators call the health 'industry'. It is not the intention to provide anything other than the barest details required to disclose something of the extent to which the health system is dysfunctional. Those interested in an history of health care provision in South Africa, could do worse than to start with Coovadia *et al* (2009), a text to which we shall refer again below.

Table 5 gives an indication of the ways in which access to health care is obtained in South Africa. About 15 per cent use solely private sector care: a further 21 per cent

---

[110] Their analysis for the most recent period (Swart *et al*, 2008, p.130) is based on the data in the 2005 National Food Consumption Survey – Fortification Baseline (Labadarios *et al*, 2008). Another set of estimates, this time from South Africa's *Millennium Development Goals Country Report 2010* (Stats SA, 2011a, p.32), based on figures from the District Health Information System, gives a national incidence of severe malnutrition among under-5s of 7.8 per cent. The worst was the 13.3 per cent in KwaZulu-Natal; the Eastern Cape came in at 8.1 per cent (after Gauteng, these are South Africa's most populous provinces, home to about 35 per cent of the total population). Least bad was the Western Cape at 3.8 per cent.

appear to consult private sector practitioners for minor problems, but revert to the public sector for major problems.[111] Almost two-thirds of the population relies entirely on the public sector. Although the quality of private sector care tends to approach that available in much-developed economies,[112] the figures for expenditure are pushed up by the high costs of hospital and specialist (consultant) fees, implying that costs alone are not a good indicator of quality.[113] Health outcomes in the different provinces vary considerably, with poverty, or socio-economic status, being a major determinant.

Table 5 Comparative expenditure – private and public health care

	Proportion of population (%)	Annual expenditure per beneficiary	Proportion of total health care expenditure (%)
Private sector medical schemes	15	R9500 ($1170)	46
Out-of-pocket primary care, public sector hospital care	21	R1500 ($185)	
All public sector health care	64	R1300 ($160)	
Source: Coovadia *et al*, 2009, pp.9-10. Results are for the year 2005			

Table 6 presents a number of development indicators in three provinces – the Western Cape, although relatively wealthy, has a rapidly growing African population, attracted mainly from the very poor Eastern Cape, by superior service delivery and the possibilities of employment. Crowded into squatter settlements, many a long way from employment opportunities and basic services, conditions for many of these migrants are appalling. KwaZulu-Natal has a solid industrial base and fairly large white and Indian populations. For many of the more numerous Africans, especially in rural areas, conditions are also bad. As may be seen, by whatever any indicator one chooses, people are best-off in the Western Cape.

---

[111] A preliminary study by Geldenhuis (2008?) of the 2002/2003 WHS data for South Africa suggests that inadequate private insurance (medical aid) protection can have catastrophic consequences in the event of a major episode of ill-health, pushing larger, relatively well-off households, in particular, into impoverishment, or poorer ones deeper into poverty.
[112] Benatar (2004, p.82) notes that "In practical terms, the disparities [between public and private healthcare] are illustrated by the fact that, nationally, there are 8.7 cardiac surgeons per 1 million population who perform 774 operations per 1 million people annually in the private sector; in the public sector, there are 0.6 cardiac surgeons per 1 million people who perform 69 operations per 1 million population."
[113] There was talk of an inquiry into the sector. See the article "Competition Commission may probe healthcare" by Amanda Visser in *Business Day*, 30 December 2011.

Table 6 Health and development indicators, 2008

Province	Western Cape	Eastern Cape	KwaZulu-Natal
Living below poverty (<R250 month; %). 2005	10	29	33
Access to free potable water within 200m (%) 2006	91	50	62
Infant mortality rate per 1000 live births, 2007	25	60	60
Adult mortality (probability of dying 15-60, %), 2007	37	60	72
Public sector doctors per 100 000 uninsured pop, 2007	34	17	30
Public sector budget per head, 2007-2008	1933	1290	1508
Covered by medical schemes (%), 2006	24	9	11
Tuberculosis cure rate (%), 2005	72	54	45
Delivery rate in facility (%), 2006	92	65	78
Source: Coovadia, 2009, p.10			

Despite successes in fixing the mess left behind by apartheid, huge problems remain (Coovadia, 2009). Counted among the successes are: the unifying of a fragmented system (the failed bantustan project of dividing South Africa into a 'white' state with four provinces and nine or ten black 'independent' states, bequeathed 14 departments of health to the democratic government); shifting expenditure away from hospitals (80 per cent of total expenditure in 1994), with academic and other tertiary hospitals accounting for 44 per cent of total expenditure, to primary care clinics (more than 1400 built) and 300 renovated, and making primary care available to users at no cost (Coovadia, 2009, pp.12).[114]

---

[114] Vital as the shift in emphasis from tertiary care to primary was, in the process of making the transition, severe damage was done to the former. The irony is that as the reach of primary care began to expand, the numbers of referrals to the big teaching hospitals began to increase, while at the same time, the capacity of these hospitals was being significantly reduced. The tale of what happened to Groote Schuur, the public sector hospital affiliated to the University of Cape Town's medical faculty, is instructive. Here is part of the story, as told by Benatar (2004, pp.84). "Between 1995 and 2000, the public health sector in the Western Cape was downsized by 3601 hospital beds (24.4 percent) and by 9282 health and support personnel (27.9 percent), while the local population increased by 8 percent. At Groote Schuur Hospital, cardiac surgical operations in adults have been reduced from 700 per year to fewer than 250 per year. In the orthopedics department, budgetary reductions have resulted in the limitation of joint replacements to 60 procedures per year in 2003, as compared with 350 in 1993. In the ophthalmology department, there has been a 60 percent reduction in faculty and a 50 percent reduction in beds over the past decade. In the general surgery department, the waiting time for surgery for breast cancer is now 8 weeks (as compared with a wait of 2 weeks 10 years ago). A reduction in neurosurgical facilities has required the withdrawal of intensive treatment from those patients who have been given the

Set against these achievements, however, are a string of failures, some of them catastrophic. Not the least of these was Ministerial incompetence and presidential interference.[115] Official obstructiveness has declined considerably and willingness

---

worst prognoses. … The number of full-time faculty members in the department of medicine was reduced from 43 in 1990 to 27 in 2003, resulting in fewer general physicians and a loss of both critical mass and experience in several subspecialties, as had been anticipated." The burden of this reduction in the quality of service did not fall upon those who could afford private healthcare.

[115] By whatever measure one cares to examine, the Eastern Cape is a deeply troubled. Several years ago, dire conditions in hospitals in the East London area, exposed after an investigation lasting several weeks by reporters from the *Daily Dispatch* (see "Why Frere's babies die", 12 July 2007), led to the dismissal of the progressive Deputy-Minister of Health, Nozizwe Madlala-Routledge. Standing in for the Minister, Dr Manto Tshabalala-Msimang (who we shall meet again below), she made an unannounced visit to the hospital immediately the report was published, declaring herself publicly to be shocked by conditions in the maternity ward. A hastily compiled report (whitewash?) commissioned by the Minister (Green-Thompson *et al*, 2007) sought to refute the newspaper's claims. Less than a month later, the Deputy-Minister was fired. A good account of the saga may be found in the blog of Acronym Required on 25 October 2007 under the heading "Public Health, AIDS, Mbeki, and the Media". Downloaded on 9 July 2012 from http://acronymrequired.com/mg/mt-search.cgi?IncludeBlogs=2&tag=Frere%20Hospital&limit=20.

It is, in fact, surprising that Madlala-Routledge lasted as long as she did. The previous year, she had incurred President Mbeki's wrath for attending an International Aids Vaccine Initiative conference in Madrid without his authorisation. No wonder he did not want her to go – her appearance grabbed international headlines. One newspaper report said that the Deputy-Minister, "… a plain-speaking 55-year-old Quaker, is being feted as a heroine by health campaigners, Aids sufferers and much of South Africa's media, for daring to end a decade of denial on the disease by the ruling African National Congress. In the space of a few weeks the deputy health minister has helped turn government policy on its head. She has publicly admitted for the first time that the government has been in "denial at the very highest level" over Aids." See the article by Stephen Bevan "African minister ends decade of denial on Aids" in the *Daily Telegraph*, 11 Dec 2006. Another article showing clearly why she was unlikely to have endeared herself to the President and the Minister of Health (close comrades and allies on whom we shall have more to say below for their infamous conduct of the fight against HIV/AIDS) had appeared in the *Telegraph* a week earlier in which her criticisms of the duo were freely aired. See "S Africa launches 'no sex' message to cut Aids", 4 December 2006.

Five years on, the troubles in the Eastern Cape refuse to go away. On 4 July 2012, for example, under the heading "Reaction over whistle-blowing doctors", the *Cape Times* carried a report by Etienne Creux about clinical heads of specialised units in provincial hospitals going to the press to publicise a "… shortage of doctors and other staff … so serious they would have to limit the services offered, such as offering only life-saving and

to tackle health system problems, many of government's own making, increased markedly with the appointment, first of Barbara Hogan as Minister of Health, and then about a year later, of Aaron Motsoaledi. In his maiden budget speech in June 2009, Minister Motsoaledi pointed out that:

"The public health system is ... forced to carry the ever increasing burden of diseases, obviously made worse by poverty, HIV and AIDS, and other communicable diseases....Ability to provide the necessary services is hampered by:

- lack of managerial skills within health institutions;
- failure to cut on identified deficiencies;
- delayed response to quality improvement requirements;
- unsatisfactory maintenance and repair services;
- poor technological management;
- poor supply chain management;[116]
- inability of individuals to take responsibility for their actions;
- poor disciplinary procedures and corruption;
- significant problems in clinical areas related to training and poor attitude of staff; and lastly
- inadequate staffing levels in all areas" (DoH, 2009)

If we turn to the section on health in the Appendix at the end of the present paper, we find the National Planning Commission endorsing the Minister's analysis, as in this sample of the criticism levelled at the public health sector:

"Evidence suggests multiple system failure across a range of programmes, including maternal and child health,[117] HIV/AIDS, tuberculosis and others, with a devastating combined impact. At the heart of this failure is the inability to get primary health care and the district health system to function effectively."

---

emergency surgery". Acting out of desperation after numerous appeals to the provincial and national departments of health had failed to have to produce any response, the doctors concerned now face disciplinary action.

[116] Once more, there are dozens of newspaper articles giving an insight into the problem. See, for example, the piece by Katlego Moeng in *The Sowetan*, 25 November 2011, "Gauteng Health faces crisis over R300m debt". See also Bateman, 2009a.

[117] The literature on the heartbreakingly sad toll exacted in South Africa by maternal mortality and child death, much of it preventable by simple methods, is huge, as it should be. One of the more arresting titles on the former topic to appear in recent times is *Stop Making Excuses* (Human Rights Watch, 2011). Measuring child and maternal mortality is difficult. For an introduction see Nicol and Bradshaw (2010)

The draft human resource strategy for the health sector for the period 2012/2013 to 2016/2017, compiled by the Department of Health, concludes starkly that:

> *"The evidence is that South Africa's performance in terms of health outcomes when compared with peer countries is extremely poor*, with much higher infant and maternal mortality. This reflects on poor productivity, poor design and poor management of resources and not only necessarily on the number of available professionals in the health sector."[118] (DoH, 2011, p.28, emphasis in original)

The volume of evidence in support of this, and other similar analyses of the causes of the crisis in public health care, is overwhelming – not much of it need be reproduced here – it is sufficient for our purposes that the Minister of Health and the Minister of National Planning are broadly in agreement about the depth and causes of the problems. Of more importance at this point is the question of whether Alkire and her co-workers, knowing that the health dimension is difficult to measure, should not have considered the possibility of corroborating the conclusions they had drawn (on the basis of two output measures), by looking at the quality of health sector inputs, and the efficiency of the processes by which these are turned into desired outputs.

By restricting the scope of their inquiry into the state of health to the assessment of just two outputs, child mortality and malnutrition or malnourishment, Alkire and Santos fail to see the bigger picture, namely, the crisis in the healthcare sector and its implications for health outcomes. On any examination of the abundant evidence, it is clear that inputs and processes are at the heart of that crisis (as, of course, is the socio-economic status of the most afflicted). Alkire's and Santos' position with respect to the use of inputs is cautious. Discussing living standard indicators, for example, they remark that:

> "We are aware that [… they] are means rather than ends; they are not direct measures of funtionings (*sic*). Yet, they have two strengths. In the first place, unlike income, which can serve an incredibly wide range of purposes (and one

---

[118] The question of appropriate staffing levels is a vexed one. The health department's human resource strategy referred to above looks at the issue in some depth. Noting that South Africa system may be described as a 'nurse-based public healthcare system', it informs readers that of 20 000 establishment posts for doctors, 4400 were unfilled (DoH, 2011, p.26). Crisp (2011) also takes a critical look at the question of personnel shortages in the health services. Every so often, true horror stories surface. An example, published in the *South African Medical Journal*, citing annual reports, drew attention to the official claim that "… the average of medical specialist vacancies at Pietermaritzburg and Durban's tertiary hospitals stands at 70% and 63% respectively. Medical officer vacancies at the two hospital complexes are 28% and 63% respectively." (Bateman, 2009b, p.76)

never knows whether it is used effectively to accomplish the needs considered to be basic), these are means very closely connected to the end (functioning) they are supposed to facilitate." (2010a, p.16)

As an argument in favour of the use of living standard indicators, this seems impeccable. Using inputs in the health care sector as indicators is, however, more complex. Before jumping into the arena, though, and into related questions about process, Alkire and Santos could, since they used the WHS as their primary data source for the construction of the 2003 South African MPI, have trawled through the survey looking for signs of respondent dissatisfaction with the service. Although it is necessary to be wary when attempting to take 'dissatisfaction' into account in the design of policy, questions that pick up telltale signs of the possibility/likelihood of the crisis in the health sector, ought not to be ignored. Section 7 of the WHS Individual questionnaire (questions 7000-7510) looks at 'Health System Responsiveness', gathering a vast amount of information as it goes. Consider for a moment the following question:

"Q7021 In general would you say you are very satisfied, fairly satisfied, neither satisfied nor dissatisfied, fairly dissatisfied or very dissatisfied with the way health care runs in your country." (WHO, 2002b)

Detailed analysis of the section 7 questions in the WHS (and the section 8 ones as well, for good measure), would seem to be good idea. In addition to a large number of questions about the health system, the WHS also makes use of a series of vignettes (stories about people's experience with the health services) to which individuals surveyed are invited to respond.[119] All things considered, it would seem that potentially, the WHS is capable of revealing, if not crisis, then at least the existence of high degrees of dissatisfaction, a possible manifestation of serious structural problems in the health system.[120]

Once the WHS has been thoroughly milked, however, a move to a much more sophisticated approach, one that takes account of inputs, processes and outputs in assessing the efficacy of the healthcare system, would be necessary. Analysing the efficiency of a health system is not a task for the faint-hearted. For a taste of the

---

[119] Rice *et al* (2009) look at aspects of the validity of the vignette approach, confirming its usefulness.

[120] The absence of serious dissatisfaction cannot necessarily be taken to mean that all is well – is it possible that some of the people who have never before enjoyed the privilege of health care at district level may not yet have reached the point where they perceive the quality of service to be poor? Although it is probably sensible to be a bit pessimistic about what the WHS may reveal, it does seem necessary to work through the data to see what is there.

complexity of such an enterprise, readers are invited to chew on a recent OECD working paper on the topic (Joumard *et al*, 2010). The work deserves to be read if only as a primer on the difficulties of performing such tests. Having done so, I suspect that there will be few takers for a repeat performance in low- and middle-income countries.

That being the case, our attempt to discover whether or not Alkire and Santos could have found evidence of the crisis in South Africa's healthcare services relying solely on survey data, limps to an end. The mere act of writing such a sentence, however, makes it clear that placing all one's eggs in a single survey basket is daft. Before performing any operation on the WHS database, Alkire and Santos should have consulted the literature on both the state of the healthcare services, and the patterns of morbidity and mortality, as well as that on malnutrition in South Africa. Doing so would, in all probability, have warned them of the dangers of relying on their chosen indicators, regardless of how well these perform elsewhere.

With that, we turn to the other catastrophe that their choice of indicators rendered invisible – the HIV/AIDS curse and its deadly companion, TB, including the multi-drug resistant type (MRT) in South Africa.

Coping with epidemics in a highly unequal society

It has been claimed above that part of the reason why the Alkire *et al* attempts to estimate the value of the health dimension in the MPI are so weak is because the mortality indicator they have chosen (Child mortality – If any child has died in the family) is inappropriate. If HIV/AIDS were a condition that affected only the well-off, the weakness of a mortality indicator that overlooks the death of more than two million adults in a decade, would not be of much consequence to the business of estimating MPIs. Although prevalence rates by socio-economic status (SES) do not appear to be available, it is, however, certainly not true that the poor are unaffected by it. What we do not know and cannot easily discover, is how many of the poor and the ultra-poor, or those suffering multiple deprivations, are among the sufferers. The objective of the exploration of the HIV/AIDS literature that follows is to see what that literature has to say about the incidence of this plague.

From the early-1990s onwards, the HIV/AIDS epidemic in South Africa, as elsewhere, gathered force. Exacerbated by years of shameful denialism emanating from the Presidency,[121] the numbers testing positive for HIV leapt, with about four

---

[121] Denial of the causal link between HIV and AIDS.

million infected by the year 2000.[122] Treatment of AIDS with anti-retroviral drugs did not commence on a mass scale until about 2005. By then, as may be seen in Table 7, the prevalence rate among women of reproductive age had climbed to an estimated 17 per cent, while the total number estimated to be HIV-positive was said to be about 4.2 million. The number of adults receiving anti-retroviral treatment (ART) in 2000 amounted to a little over 100 000. Five years later in 2010, when the female prevalence rate had passed the 18 per cent mark, and the HIV population had climbed to 4.7 million, the number receiving ART had increased almost tenfold to 1.06 million.[123]

In creating the estimates in Table 7, Statistics South Africa was obliged to make a host of assumptions.[124] One of the assumptions of interest to us here deals with life expectancy after becoming infected, or, more precisely: "… the median time from HIV infection to death… ", namely "… 10.5 years for men and 11.5 years for women." This is "… in line with the UNAIDS Reference Group recommendation… "[125] With finer-grained data on the age distribution, it is a simple matter to make plausible guesses at the years of life lost to this scourge. [126]

---

[122] Thurlow *et al* estimate that the national prevalence rate was about 0.16 per cent in 1990; 3.42 per cent in 1995, and 13.16 per cent in 2000 (2009, Table 2, p.2)

[123] See Stats SA, 2011c, Table 3, p.4.

[124] Four variables are assumed to decline steadily from 2001 or 2002 onwards – the crude birth rate (from 26.1 to 21.0 per 1000); the total fertility rate (from 2.9 to 2.4); the infant mortality rate (from 53.3 to 37.9), and the under-five mortality rate (from 78.8 to 54.3). The year 2005 is a turning point for the fall in estimates of life expectancy at birth. For men, it drops from 52.1 in 2001 to 49.6 in 2005, then rises to 54.9 in 2011. Corresponding figures for women are 57.8; 53.8, and 59.1 – the obvious impact of the greater burden of the disease on women. See Statistical release P0302, 27 July 2011 (Stats SA, 2011c) Table 5, p.6. These assumptions appear to be roughly in line with the ASSA-2008 (Actuarial Society of South Africa) results presented in Table 6 below.

[125] See Stats SA, 2011c, p.5.

[126] Although the official causes of death statistics in South Africa do not show it, the number of deaths each year attributed to HIV/AIDS (more women than men) at all ages is much greater than the number of child deaths. In 2009, of 572 673 people who are recorded as having died, 15 570 were reported as having done so of HIV disease. Tuberculosis claimed 69 003, and influenza and pneumonia a further 42 964 (See Statistical release P0309.3, 30 November 2011, p.34) (Stats SA, 2011d). According to South Africa's *MDG Country Report 2010*, HIV/TB co-infection rates in 2009 exceeded 70 per cent (Stats SA, 2011a, p.80). In 2009, the proportion of the population with advanced HIV infection with access to ARVs was 41 per cent (Statistics South Africa, 2010, p.80). For a discussion of the ASSA position on AIDS deaths, see Bradshaw *et al*, 2002. Statistical release P0309.3 reports that 37 974 children under the age of one year died, while 12 497 aged between one and four years did so as well (Stats SA, 2011d, p.18).

Table 7 HIV prevalence & numbers of people living with HIV, 2001–2010

Year	Prevalence rates			Total number of people living with HIV (in millions)
	Percentage of Women 15-49	Percentage of adult population 15-49	Percentage of the total Population	
2001	17.4	16.0	9.4	4.21
2005	18.3	16.2	9.9	4.69
2010	19.3	16.5	10.5	5.26
2011	19.4	16.6	10.6	5.80
Source: Table 4 on p.5 in Statistical release P0302, 27 July 2011 (Stats SA, 2011c).				

What this suggests is that the approach adopted by Noble *et al* (who argue that premature death is an appropriate health indicator), may hold greater promise than that adopted by Alkire and her co-workers. To measure the impact of such deaths, Noble *et al* estimate "… Years of Potential Life Lost (YPLL), the level of unexpected mortality … weighted by the age of the individual who has died… " (2006a, p.20).[127] Add to that the large number of adults who die of non-natural causes each year, many of whom meet violent deaths. Most of those who do are aged 15-49 years, and most of them are men. Under such circumstances, as a health indicator, the Noble *et al* measure surely makes more sense. It would make even more sense if the burden on the health services, already overloaded with AIDS sick, and piled on top of that, the end-result of a couple of hundred thousand instances of assault with intent to do grievous bodily harm, could be measured adequately. Notwithstanding the superiority of the YPLL, Noble and Wright (2009) were unable to estimate its value from Statistics South Africa's massive 2007 Community Survey (Stats SA, 2007) because the survey did not furnish the necessary data.[128]

---

[127] Using the figures in Table 7 above to generate a back-of-envelope estimate, we can say that if the mean age of the infected was about 30 years, and their life expectancy at birth in the absence of AIDS would have been, say, 55 years, then by dying at age 41 years, the average loss would have been about 14 years per person. Multiply this by the five million or so of those living with HIV, and out pops a loss of 70 million life years. One is aware, in making speculations of this sort, that the results yielded by the counterfactuals employed, need to be tested for sensitivity. The international benchmark age used when estimating YPLL is 75years. See Noble *et al*, 2006a, p.58.

[128] As noted above, Alkire and Santos (2010a) also eschewed use of the 2007 Community Survey because it lacked nutrition data and because the mortality data were inadequate.

Yet Table 7 tells us that HIV/AIDS cannot possibly be ignored. Under such circumstances, what is to be done? That being so, a question that must be addressed is that of the extent to which the authorities (and the broader research community) are knowledgeable about the relationship between HIV/AIDS and poverty (answering this question makes it possible to begin to assess the implications of government inaction due to ignorance). In the South African case, the answer is that although the dimensions of that relationship cannot be spelled out with precision, quite a lot is known about the problem, especially the HIV/AIDS part of it. A long and ultimately victorious struggle against denialism and official prejudice over the issue of the use of anti-retrovirals to treat the AIDS sick,[129] was fought by a well-informed activist group, making good use of the knowledge gained from the huge amount of research in the field. Although formidable, the difficulties faced in constructing plausible estimates of the extent of the problem, are not so intractable as to cause paralysis – once a set of assumptions like those used to create the national estimates in Table 7 have been made, they can be refined through debate.

The debate has been vigorous and, at times, quite rancorous. A major contributor to the discussion, the Actuarial Society of South Africa (ASSA), has constructed an open access model that allows for the estimation of a wide range of variables of interest. Now in its *n*th iteration, ASSA2008 has recently been released. Like its predecessors, the model allows knowledgeable users to change certain assumptions. The base-line estimates published by ASSA make it possible, however, for the casual user to learn quite a lot about the problem.

Taking figures from the ASSA model allows the user to peep into hell, as Table 8 illustrates. The results presented here, taken from the latest version of the model (ASSA 2008),[130] suggest that the model it replaces, the ASSA 2003, overstated the severity of the problem somewhat, primarily because of assumptions made at the time about the efficacy of the anti-AIDS campaign.

---

[129] Strong support for President Mbeki's stance came from the late Dr. Tshabalala-Msimang (a medical doctor), who served as Minister of Health in South Africa from 1999 until Mbeki was forced out of office in 2008. Describing HIV/AIDS as a disease of poverty, she argued for the use of vitamin and improved nutrition, using foods like garlic, lemon, African potatoes and beetroot, downplaying the importance of ART by frequent reference to its toxicity. For this, she was widely derided, earning the sobriquet of Dr Beetroot. While it cannot be denied that poor nutrition is a public health issue and one of paramount importance, the resistance to the roll-out of ART on a national basis, and the foot-dragging after the decision was finally taken in 2002 to do so, have seen accusations levelled against her and Mbeki of being responsible for hundreds of thousands of unnecessary deaths (Coovadia *et al*, 2009, p.15).

[130] See http://aids.actuarialsociety.org.za/ASSA2008-Model-3480.htm. Accessed 23 November 2011.

Table 8 HIV/AIDS in South Africa 2000-2011: Selected indicators

Year	2000	2011
Total population	45 255 267	50 840 589
Total HIV infections	2 977 995	5 577 812
Total births	1 147 110	1 059 462
Births infected perinatally	42 560	23 385
Babies newly infected by mother's milk	25 711	19 562
Total fertility rate	2.94	2.39
AIDS sick		
Total AIDS sick (in the middle of year)	169 728	519 214
Deaths[131]		
Non-AIDS deaths (in the year starting 1 July)	378 769	411 506
AIDS deaths (in the year starting 1 July)	118 037	187 758
Accumulated Aids Deaths (to middle of the year)	242 362	2 572 448
Prevalence rates		
Adults aged 15 – 49	11.4%	17.0%
Total population	6.6%	11.0%
Incidence rates		
Total population	1.51%	0.72%
Total new infections	636 716	324 307
Mortality statistics		
Infant mortality rate	52	34
Under 5 mortality rate	72	49
Life expectancy at birth	58.3	58.4
Maternal orphan statistics		
Total orphans	706 385	1 712 677
Total AIDS orphans	121 747	1 264 771
New orphans	134 273	192 153

Source: ASSA-2008
Note: The incidence rate is the number of new infections in a given population within a specific time period. The relevant populations are those at the head of each column. The time period is one year.

---

[131] The ASSA mortality estimates and those released by Statistics South Africa for the year 2010/2011 are within about 30 000 of each other, a tolerable error of about five cent. See Stats SA, 2011d. The 2005 HSRC AIDS survey, however, detected many more orphans than ASSA. According to the HSRC, in 2005 there were 2.5 million orphans in South Africa, 456 000 maternal orphans, 1.75 million paternal orphans and 330 000 double orphans (Shisana *et al*, 2005, p.112).

As ART started to work in earnest, life expectancy has risen as infection rates have fallen.[132] The good news is that despite an increasing prevalence rate, perinatal infections and mother's milk infections fell; in addition, the incidence rate, and hence the number of new infections during the year 2011, fall. Infant mortality rates and under-5 mortality rates drop substantially.

On the other side of the balance sheet, the number of AIDS sick trebles; AIDS deaths increase by about 59 per cent, while non-AIDS deaths only grow by about nine per cent, accumulated deaths in an 11-year period exceed 2.5 million, and finally, the total number of maternal orphans increases more than tenfold. Be the property of decomposability never so attractive, the MPI as presently constituted, simply does not have the ability to draw attention to a human tragedy of these proportions.

Administrative data from hospitals and clinics can provide both a reality check on provincial-level estimates, as well the basic data required for budgetary allocations. How effectively these data are gathered is not at issue here (the likelihood is that the processes are hampered by numerous obstacles, bureaucratic incompetence and bungling being high on the list). The point rather is that external warnings in the form of mashup indices of the sort offered by the UNDP cannot contribute much to the solution of these problems, even if that contribution is intended to be the limited one of bringing to the attention of the authorities the fact that some proportion of the population is suffering chronic multi-dimensional poverty, in which health deprivation significant.

Not only has the MPI got nothing of value to add to the debate on AIDS in South Africa, unless its creators can design and implement a special survey, an expanded version of a national survey thus far carried out on three occasions in the country (Shisana and Simbayi et al, 2002; Shisana et al, 2005; Shisana et al, 2009, on which, more below), the chances of its being able to 'isolate' any part of this complex and important reality are negligibly small. This, as noted above, is because prevalence data by socio-economic status (SES) are not available (and are difficult to obtain using surveys).

---

[132] In the likely event that the burden of HIV/AIDS on the poor was heavy, neither dire conditions in 2003, nor any sign of these welcome improvements, could be detected by the Alkire and Santos health indicators. Recall here their boast, cited above, that: "The Alkire Foster method reflects other dimensions directly and changes immediately as these change. This makes it an effective monitoring tool because improvements in the dimensions measured, such as health and education, are reflected quickly."

'Policy relevance' depends to some extent on the use to which information gathered is to be put. For purposes of policy evaluation, one can readily extract prevalence rates, numbers of AIDS sick and mortality figures on a national and provincial basis from an instrument such as the ASSA model. As long as the model is kept healthy on a regular diet of fresh reliable data, its outputs could provide a rough measure of the efficacy of policies devised and implemented to deal with the reality of HIV/AIDS. Finding or creating 'policy relevant' tools for estimating the costs of dealing with the epidemic would be another matter altogether. Huge demands are made on medical and social resources to cope with a disaster on the scale of the epidemic in South Africa.

If zero-base estimates were required of the cost of providing care for the HIV-infected while they live, and estimates of what it might cost to give support to those they leave behind them when die, the difficulty of obtaining prevalence data by socio-economic status, would constitute an almost insuperable barrier.[133] Fortunately for the National Treasury, budgeting from a zero baseline is not required – extrapolations, modified by the latest information on the impact and progress of the disease, are probably sufficient (even if only barely so).

Progress beyond this point in the direction of evidence of a connection between HIV/AIDS and the much-deprived, becomes more difficult. There is a huge literature on HIV/AIDS in South Africa – a search through it, again, a little cursory, has so far failed to throw up the seminal paper that one hopes has been written on the subject of income-specific prevalence rates. Let us take a small digression into the field to see how much can be learned from what is readily available.

---

[133] Zero-based budgeting to meet the costs of providing the country's relatively generous (disability) grants to the AIDS sick, would be a nightmare (fortunately, it does not have to be carried out!). The value of South Africa's disability grant in 2008 was R940 per month. This represented 130 per cent of household expenditure in the bottom decile of households; 80 per cent in the second decile, and 60 per cent in the third decile (Stats SA, 2011b, pp.132ff). Such 'generosity' is argued to constitute a powerful perverse incentive. Following WHO guidelines, HIV positive people qualify for temporary disability grants when their CD4 lymphocyte count falls below 200 cells per cubic millilitre of blood. Reports exist of grant recipients attempting to manipulate CD4 levels so as to remain below the cutoff point, and thus continue to qualify for the grant (de Paoli et al, 2010, pp.13-14). It has also been estimated that the grant is possibly responsible for labour participation rates being up to 25 per cent lower than they would have been in the absence of grants (Mutasa, 2010). How useful such a claim is in a country where the official unemployment rate is estimated to hover in the region of 25 per cent is not immediately obvious.

Searching for the AIDS/poverty nexus

For a variety of reasons, HIV status is not something that people are keen to disclose publicly. Despite guarantees of confidentiality, many surveys cannot elicit credible responses to questions on the subject. Sometimes, the respondent in a household survey simply does not know the status of all household members. More likely, however, is that concern about the stigma attaching to AIDS discourages disclosure. This was certainly the case with South Africa's General Household Survey (GHS) – for years, it yielded absurdly low estimates of the numbers of 'People Living with HIV' (PLWH) – its attempts to measure substance abuse enjoyed the same fate. Because of this, and because cause of death statistics also seriously under-record AIDS deaths (let alone capture any information about income), income-specific HIV/AIDS rates are rare. In South Africa, only the first one of three HSRC studies referred to above (at which we shall glance below), attempted, without great success, to look at socio-economic status (SES). Subsequent HSRC surveys steered clear of the matter.

In the absence of a definitive study on the relationship between HIV/AIDS and poverty, the question of how to proceed arises. The approach adopted here is to use hypotheses on poverty and HIV/AIDS in South Africa tested by Tladi (2006), as a guide to the possible shape of the relationship in question. These are subjected to (a rough and ready) test by comparing predicted relationships with reported relationships between income levels and Years of Potential Life Lost (YPLL) in the early Noble *et al* papers (2006a and 2006b). These are the papers giving estimates of the Provincial Indices of Multiple Deprivation for the year 2001 (PIMDs).

The next step is to scour the first HSRC study of HIV/AIDs (Shisana and Simbayi *et al*, 2002) to see what support if any, it provides for the Tladi hypotheses. A sidelong glance is then taken at a few pieces that floated to the surface to see what empirical evidence they offer. One of these is the 2003 HDR for South Africa (UNDP, 2003). The voyage as a whole ends with some speculation on the limits of the range in which HIV/AIDS prevalence rates for very poor people may lie, obtained by the use of a simple simulator. The outcome is a set of guesses at what HIV/AIDS prevalence rates, and numbers affected, may be among the poor and the very poor.

The Tladi hypotheses

What causes people to behave in ways that result in their becoming HIV positive is complex, and certainly not to be understood in terms of a few socio-economic variables (although this has not prevented economists from attempting to do so). This does not necessarily mean that people's material conditions have no influence on their behaviour; rather, it means that no simple relationships have been uncovered. The literature is vast – there is a good summary in a paper by Holmqvist (2009) – Table 1 in the Holmqvist paper adapts the work of Barnett and Whiteside (2006) to produce a set of linkages between HIV and its potential determinants. There are two sets of distal (macro- and micro-environments) and two sets of proximal (behaviour and biology) determinants, each column containing five separate determinants (2009, p.3). Holmqvist's main interest in is the question of whether or not there is a link between HIV and income inequality, and if so, what it would tell us? En route to an attempt at answering the question, we are offered stories from different disciplines: economics (utility maximisation); sociology (social capital and trust); political economy (public service); history (decolonisation). Each has a little to contribute – none is conclusive. One important finding, albeit tentative, is that:

"… HIV is not robustly related to poverty. Africa is poor and has high HIV prevalence, but neither within Africa nor among the non-African developing countries does poverty emerge as being significantly related to HIV." (Holmqvist, 2009, p.8)

Holmqvist concludes that there is a "significant and robust" link between income inequality and HIV, but he admits to being unable to explain why "unequal societies [should be] more vulnerable to HIV?" (p.19). As a highly unequal society, one with extremes of wealth and poverty, and one moreover, that has only recently been 'decolonised', South Africa is clearly of great interest. Although this looks like a fruitful area for research, I want to turn instead to a less ambitious project, one that set out to explore HIV risk by income category. Tladi (2006) set out to test the following hypothesis:

 "Poor individuals are more susceptible to HIV infection than their non-poor counterparts, for the following reasons:

- poverty and its associated factors, such as low education, reduce the chances of the poor having good knowledge of the means of preventing HIV infection
- poor women are less likely to use condoms or to negotiate condom use due to both low education levels and economic dependence on their partners." (2006, p.372)

Data for the study was from the South African Demographic and Health Survey (SADHS) of 1998. The sample consisted of 12 000 women aged between 15 and 49 years. Poverty status as measured by income level, was either 'very poor' (R0-600 per month); 'poor' (R601-1000 per month), or 'non-poor' (R1001 or more per month). The claim that:

> "… the poor were less likely to adopt safer sexual behaviour due to low levels of education and financial dependence on their partners, which reduce their sexual negotiating power …. was supported by the results of the data analysis which showed that the non-poor were more likely to use condoms than the very poor. As with knowledge of the effective means of avoiding HIV infection, the chances of having used a condom during last sexual intercourse improved with an increase in the level of education attained.
>
> The relationship between economic status and sexual behavioural practices is perhaps better reflected by the association between economic status and non-use of condoms as a result of a partner's dislike of condoms. Respondents who received money from their partners, as well as those who came from households where hunger was a common phenomenon, were more likely not to use condoms because their partners dislike them than those who did not, that is, controlling for level of education and economic status, among other factors."

Another interesting aspect of her work is the differences found between the conduct of the poor and the very poor. Reporting her findings in this regard, she says that the:

> "… results demonstrate the intricacy of the poverty and HIV/AIDS relationship, whereby it is not only low economic status that increases susceptibility to HIV infection but also high socio-economic status. While being poor increases susceptibility much more than being non-poor, the stigmatisation of HIV/AIDS as a disease of poverty, which provides the poor with a false sense of protection from HIV infection, may hinder their adoption of safer sexual behaviours. This is evidenced by the increased odds of non-use of condoms due to low perceived risk of HIV infection among the poor compared with the very poor and among those who never experienced hunger as opposed to those who came from households where hunger was frequent and even among the white population (which has few poor people) as opposed to blacks." (Tladi, 2006, p.380)

In a field in which there are not many studies of this nature, her findings offer some guidance in the construction of the simple simulator model whose results are presented at the end of this section. The categories used to distinguish 'very poor' from 'poor' from 'non-poor' (p.372) are such that the latter form a huge residual among whom different attitudes to the risk of HIV infection are likely to be found. Our ignorance (at this point) about attitudes among the non-poor groups, guards against any temptation to posit a simple monotonic relationship leading from somewhat risk-averse behaviour at the very bottom of the income distribution, through fairly lax behaviour among the poor, to similar behaviour among sections of the non-poor.

The imaginative leap necessary to get from poverty to multiple deprivation is not all that large – if the Tladi results are reliable, we would expect the correlation between deprivation in the income domain and health domains, to be positive but far from perfect.[134] Let us see what the work of Noble *et al* has to say on the matter.

Years of Potential Life Lost

In the 2001 PIMDs, Noble *et al*, managed to make use of the mortality data in the 2001 population census to estimate Years of Potential Life Lost (YPLL). As noted above, however, they were not able to repeat this when it came to updating their earlier estimates making use of the data in the 2007 Community Survey.[135] If we can learn anything useful from their work about the relationship between deprivation in the health and income domains (dimensions), it is going to be necessary to make use of the 2001 PIMDs. This information may be 'old', but it is not insignificant – although AIDS deaths increased rapidly after 2001,[136] they were sufficient in number in 2001 to have made a substantial impact on estimates of YPLL (i.e., YPLL should have been significantly higher in 2001 than it had been a decade earlier).

Analysis of the 2001 data allows the onlooker to gain a glimmering of an understanding of how complex the relationship is between early death and the other domains. Table 9 gives their estimates of the correlation between health deprivation and the other four domains, as well as the correlation between health deprivation and the Indices of Multiple Deprivation.

Apart from the Limpopo province, the correlation between health deprivation and the PIMD is reasonably high. Income deprivation is important, but not overwhelmingly so. With two exceptions, the Eastern Cape and Gauteng, deprivations in other domains show little clear relationship with each other. In the

---

[134] The Tladi project made use of the 1998 Demographic and Health Survey data for South Africa. Although the data are somewhat old, the choice of year is not a bad one, because it records attitudes at a time when the HIV/AIDS epidemic was beginning to gather increasing momentum, but before the effects of the mass campaigns to educate people had become noticeable.

[135] Alkire and Santos, it may be recalled, made use of the much smaller WHS because the Community Survey could not provide them with the necessary data on child mortality and nutrition (2010a, p22n).

[136] Table 7 tells us that in the year 2000, for every AIDS death, there were 3.2 non-AIDS deaths. By 2011, this had fallen to 2.2.

latter two, however, the standard markers of poverty, income, education, and living environment deprivation all point to the likelihood of a close connection between poverty and early death. Although it cannot be said that these results confirm the Tladi hypotheses, it can be said that they do not contradict them.

Table 9 Health domain correlations (Spearman's rho) – other domains & the PIMD

	Income deprivation	Employment deprivation	Education deprivation	Living environment deprivation	PIMD
Western Cape	0.678	0.403	0.474	0.573	0.771
Eastern Cape	0.667	0.560	0.626	0.679	0.790
Northern Cape	0.523	0.462	0.428	0.266	0.676
Free State	0.537	0.575	0.305	0.422	0.697
KwaZulu-Natal	0.545	0.495	0.463	0.478	0.674
N West Province	0.602	0.492	0.535	0.283	0.715
Gauteng	0.688	0.719	0.614	0.464	0.787
Mpumalanga	0.504	0.379	0.494	0.334	0.638
Limpopo	0.292	0.043*	0.240	0.156	0.456

Source: Noble *et al* 2006b, pp.27ff
Note: All correlations are significant at the 0.01 level (2-tailed) except where indicated by *

The Mandela-HSRC survey

One of the few surveys to rely on direct testing for HIV status (for respondents who agree to be tested), that by Shisana and Simbayi *et al* (2002, p.54), by now a little dated,[137] suggests that the poor, even if not the most heavily burdened by the epidemic in terms of absolute numbers affected, certainly cannot escape its awful clutches. The survey from which this (tentative) conclusion may be drawn used "linked anonymous saliva HIV tests" on a sample of about 10 000 (whittled down from a potential 14 000) of whom about 89 per cent agreed to an HIV test. One of the aims of the study was to identify the:

---

[137] Reference was made above to the two follow-up surveys conducted by the HSRC (Shisana *et al*, 2005 and 2009). Neither report attempts to deal with poverty in relation to HIV/AIDS, possibly because of the difficulties experienced in the 2002 survey, some of which are discussed below.

"… social, economic, political, structural and cultural contexts within which behavior occurs" (2002, p.9).

Table 10 shows prevalence rates of HIV for persons age 15 years and older by race. The measure of household disposable income is loose – without knowing what controls were in place to prevent it being overwhelmed by subjectivity,[138] it is not obvious how much trust should be placed in the results it has generated.

Table 10 HIV prevalence by household income by race, South Africa 2002

Income	Whole sample	African	White	Coloured	Indian
Not enough money for basics	13.9 (11.9-15.9)	14.5 (12.4-16.7)	6.2 (0.0-15.4)	7.6 (2.6-12.7)	1.9 (0.0-4.5)
Enough money for basics, short for others	14.0 (11.6-16.4)	16.1 (13.2-19.0)	6.4 (0.0-13.1)	4.4 (2.6-6.2)	3.7 (0.0-9.8)
Enough money for most important things	6.5 (3.7-9.3)	9.4 (3.7-15.1)	3.7 (0.9-6.4)	7.8 (1.4-14.1)	0.5 (0.0-1.3)
Some money for extras	5.0 (1.8-8.1)	10.3 (0.0-20.7)	4.6 (0.7-7.1)	2.7 (0.0-7.1)	0.0
Source: Shisana and Simbayi *et al*, 2002, Table 23, p.54. Note: The figures in parentheses demarcate the 95 per cent confidence interval. Prevalence rates are for those aged 15 years and more.					

Taking the income categories at face value for the sample as a whole, and ignoring the significant overlap in confidence intervals, prevalence rates are generally highest in the second income category (Enough money for basics, short for others), falling thereafter, i.e., the probability of being HIV positive falls as income rises. Africans bear the brunt of the epidemic, both in relative terms and in absolute terms, for not only are their prevalence rates the highest by far, they account for about 80 per cent of the total population.

Noting that the study cannot claim to have measured poverty adequately, the findings on the relationship between "… socio-economic status (a proxy measure for poverty)"and HIV suggest that among the African population, all groups are at risk. This is not the case among other races, where "… lower socio-economic status appears to be related to higher likelihood of HIV infection, even after multivariate

---

[138] Of course, surveys always depend on respondents reporting as accurately as possible. When questions are loosely worded (one person's 'basic' is another's luxury), the reliability of the survey is brought into question.

adjustment." (2002, p.63). Shisana and Simbayi *et al* thus conclude from a logit analysis that "… education and economic status were not significant independent predictors of HIV status … " (2002, p.56) – that honour goes to "… race, age, sex of respondent, [139] locality type and province of residence… "

Attempting to attach estimates of the numbers involved entails the making of fairly heroic assumptions. Since the overwhelming majority of the total population is African, we could do worse, for purposes of trying to establish a link between HIV/AIDS and poverty, than to concentrate on them. The goal is to see if we can make a plausible guess at the numbers of individuals in each of the (crudely defined) income groups in Table 10.

If the full results of the long-awaited 2008/2009 Living Conditions Survey (LCS) conducted by Statistics South Africa were available, it would be possible to extract from it a distribution of households by expenditure level, onto which could be planted the (old) prevalence rates found by Shisana and Simbayi *et al*. The expenditure data are tantalisingly out of reach. What is available from the first of the publications to emerge from the LCS, however, is a table showing that about 62 per cent of households stated that their standard of food consumption was just adequate, with 12.6 per cent stating that it was more than adequate, and 25.7 per cent that it was inadequate (Stats SA, 2011b, p.15). If we compress the four categories in Table 10 into three, we can pair them with the food consumption adequacy estimates in the LCS, then, using the prevalence rates from the HSRC study in Table 10, make a guess at how many HIV positive individuals there are in the households in the different income categories. The results of the attempt to do so are given in Table 11 below.

What with all the billions of Rand targeted at the poor since 2000 in the form mainly, of Child Support Grants and state Old Age Pensions, it would be a bit surprising if patterns of consumption adequacy were 'better' in 2002 than in 2008/2009. Using the later figures would probably not cause the number of poor in 2002 to be overstated. After climbing slowly between 2001 and 2011, HIV prevalence rates have more or less stabilised.

---

[139] It has long been known that women bear by far the heavier burden of the illness. See, for example the citation by de Paoli *et al* (2010, p.6) of an HSRC finding that "… women aged 19–25 are almost four times more likely to be HIV positive than men of this age group… ". As far as locality is concerned, urban informal settlements turn out, not surprisingly, to be the worst affected. The prevalence rate in these localities of 28 per cent of those aged between 15 and 49 years, dwarfs that in urban formal areas of 16 per cent, and that on farms of 11 per cent (Shisana and Simbayi *et al*, 2002, Figure 10, p.51).

Table 11 Distribution of HIV+ Africans by h-hold expenditure category: 2002

HSRC categories	LCS categories for food consumption expenditure	Estimate No. and Col. %	95% confidence interval Lower limit	Upper limit
Not enough money for basics	Less than adequate	918 709 28.9	786 654 37.9	1 058 099 24.6
Enough money for basics, short for others plus Enough money for most important things	Adequate	1 939 420 61.0	1 285 341 62.1	2 593 500 60.4
Some money for extras	More than adequate	319 952 10.1	0 0.0	643 010 15.0
Total numbers of households		3 178 081	2 070 996	4 294 608
Source: Own estimates based on the data and method described above. Total number of Africans aged 15 years or more = 24.65 million. This is the mid-year estimate for 2003 from Statistical release P0302, 24 July 2003, p.7.				

Using the Shisana and Simbayi *et al* rates in Table 10 should tend to understate the numbers of PLWH. Mixed well and given a gentle stir, the results suggest that were possibly 787 000 to 1.06 million PLWH in the lowest expenditure category in Table 11. A small confidence booster comes from the 2008 ASSA model in the form of the news that the total number of HIV positive folk (PLWH) in 2002 was 3.93 million, which is within the confidence interval in Table 11.[140]

Lacking any knowledge about household size by expenditure category, if we do as is done in the simulation exercise below: assume that it is about three people, then there would be somewhere between 2.4 and 3.2 million very poor people in households containing at least one HIV positive person. Apply roughly the same rules as were used in the back-of-envelope estimate with which this section commenced, and the 2003 MPI headcount could at least double.

At least at the national level, the case for the prosecution rests – the obvious avenues where one might expect to find empirical studies on the poverty/HIV relationship having been explored, there does not appear to be much more that can be done with numbers.

---

[140] At the time the HSRC results were released they were criticised by ASSA in a press released which pointed out that both small sample size and low response were problematic. In particular, the release points to the large confidence intervals associated with the former (Bennet, 2003).

South Africa's 2003 Human Development Report

The UNDP appears not to be in any no doubt about the connection between HIV/AIDS and poverty – here is what South Africa's HDR for the year 2003 had to say on the matter:

"HIV/AIDS has had a disproportionate impact on poor communities, permanently trapping many of its victims in poverty. The magnitude and far-reaching consequences of the HIV/AIDS pandemic mean that the disease is no longer a crisis only for the healthcare sector, but presents a major challenge to all sectors.

Many studies in South and southern Africa have clearly demonstrated that HIV/AIDS contributes to a rise in poverty, and that poverty reduces the ability of poor people living with HIV/AIDS to cope with the disease. AIDS generates new poverty as people lose employment and housing tenure. Household incomes fall due to the loss of wage earners and rising spending, particularly on medical care and funerals.

Not only do household outputs and incomes decline, but household members, particularly women, have to make hard choices on the allocation of their time between production, meeting household needs, child care and care of the sick.

In a recent study of 700 South African households affected by HIV/AIDS, more than half of the affected families did not have enough food to stave off starvation. Two-thirds of the households reported a loss of income as a result of the disease and larger proportions of household income being spent on health care and funerals." (UNDP, 2003, p.84)

The position of the compilers of the HDR for South Africa is unequivocal – HIV/AIDS and poverty are close companions – impoverishing those who might previously have been doing reasonably well, and pushing those who were already poor ever deeper into poverty. Unfortunately, the volume does not offer much by way of statistical information about the poverty and HIV/AIDS relationship.

Sub-national studies

If the South African HDR is found wanting (not supported by enough evidence?), and it is thought necessary to look further afield, there are several sub-national studies that throw up interesting, if partial insights into the relationship in question. One such study added bulk to the finding about prevalence rates in squatter areas, reporting that:

"… although only 9% of South Africa's population aged 2 years and over live in urban informal settlements, 29% of people living with HIV are found in these areas." (Rehle *et al*, 2007, p.199).

It is a relatively simple matter to show that when it comes to dwelling type and location, the poor in informal dwellings, either in backyards or in informal settlements are over-represented. According to the Living Conditions Survey (LCS) seven per cent of all households resided in informal dwellings,[141] not in a backyard, that is to say, in informal settlements. In the bottom expenditure decile, 17.3 per cent of all dwellings were of this type. In the second poorest decile, the proportion falls to 10.8 per cent, roughly where it is in the third poorest decile (11.3 per cent) (Stats SA, 2011b, p.152). Although there is a high probability that many of these households will be home to people living with HIV, it is not possible to say what proportion of them are, and as importantly, how many individuals are involved.

Several small-scale studies have been carried out, they vary considerably in the exoticism of the method used to analyse the data gathered or available. A study by Marzo and Murtin (2007) used a Bayesian technique to investigate AIDS illness and poverty, drawing data from a longitudinal survey that interviewed 1170 individuals in 331 households. They observe that theirs is one of the "… first attempts to analyse the impact of HIV/AIDS on poverty." (2007, p.3). Their findings highlight the existence and importance of a public safety net in the urban setting and the fragility of risk-sharing arrangements in rural areas (p.14) – interesting, but not much to take home.

Thurlow *et al* (2009) bolt a survey that took histories from 4400 workers in the four major industries in KwaZulu-Natal, onto a computable general equilibrium to estimate the economic impact of the AIDS epidemic. The model churns out prevalence rates by occupational category – unskilled workers have the highest rates but there is vigorous competition from managers and skilled workers in some sectors, replicating the Shisana and Simbayi *et al* finding that AIDS is no respecter of income.

The Thurlow *et al* study is worth citing because of its findings on the impact of HIV/AIDS on poverty. Over the long period for which the model runs (2002-2025) the poverty rate (headcount ratio) falls but little, mainly because unskilled workers, predominantly African, have higher prevalence and mortality rates. Population

---

[141] The cause of the disagreement between this figure and the estimate of nine per cent cited immediately above is not known. It has not been pursued because it is not of much significance for the argument.

growth in the working-age population being lower than growth in the population as a whole causes dependency ratios to rise. Operating counter to this is the tendency for per capita incomes to rise as household sizes fall. So, despite the greater impact of AIDS on the poor, poverty at the national level, measured in household terms does not worsen. Of course, for the households affected, the effects, as many studies attest, can be disastrous.

Vass (2005, pp.12-13) reports lower HIV prevalence rates for highly-skilled workers and managerial posts, which tend to be filled by whites. As one descends the skill ladder, the racial mix balance becomes more balanced, and prevalence rates among skilled workers, approach those reported by Thurlow *et al*.

Casale and Whitehead surveyed the literature in 2006, citing studies that show that the risk of HIV is significantly higher for individuals in poor households, and that affected households among the poor are significantly poorer (pp.4ff). Like Thurlow *et al* (2009), they also report the chilling finding that an epidemic:

"... with such severe demographic, social and human effects actually 'improves' per capita economic indicators." (p.26)[142]

A three-year project carried out in urban and peri-urban areas in the Cape Peninsula, whose aim was to examine "Poverty reduction strategies from a public health perspective; social grants, HIV/AIDS and the roll-out of HAART [highly active anti-retroviral treatment] in South Africa", used a variety of research techniques. These included two panel surveys, one looking at 216 HIV positive participants receiving ART, while the other was of a control group of 516 individuals whose HIV status was not known (de Paoli *et al*, 2010, p.8). Because most of the participants stated that unemployment and poverty were their main concerns (2010, p.10), the project's findings cannot be generalised for people living with HIV nationally. For the poor, or borderline poor, or in those households where an AIDS sick income earner is no longer able to work, the finding is that:

"Loss of the disability grant as a result of improved health had a significant impact on physical and emotional health, and led to high levels of stress. Losing the grant has direct implications for PLWHs, as a healthy diet may no longer be accessible. This in turn undermines adherence to ARVs." (de Paoli *et al*, 2010, p.12)

---

[142] Making a few more back-of-envelop speculations, I warned of the necessity to include counterfactuals about the AIDS/poverty nexus in Meth, 2011.

It is likely that this would hold true throughout the country. The policy implications of such a conclusion reach well beyond HIV/AIDS itself into the fraught question of South Africa's anti-poverty strategy. It is impossible, without increasing the thickness of an already bloated document, to wander very far into this topic. Proof, however, of the supreme importance of broadening the approach to HIV/AIDS is evident in the draft *National Strategic Plan for HIV and AIDS, STIs and TB, 2012-2016* (SANAC, 2011). Consider for a moment, the following statement:

> "Recognition of the limitations of the biomedical and anthropological/behavioural paradigms emerged when the concept of the social determinants of ill health became better understood, leading to the established and accepted paradigm of conceptualizing HIV as also a development issue. Such a concept recognizes the socio-economic context in which the epidemic occurs and the inter-relatedness of HIV with other development concerns such as poverty, inequity, lack of access to basic amenities, lack of social cohesion and many other aspects." (2011, p.34)

The Plan bristles with dozens and dozens of suggestions, recommendations and imperatives. Yet on the question of poverty, while recognising it as a major factor in the epidemics, it is powerless to utter anything other than platitudes like those above. Such a stance is by no means unreasonable – SANAC's brief is HIV/AIDS (and the others), not anti-poverty policy. The responsibility for that lies with government more broadly.

The scorecard

The wheel has come full circle – we are back with the question of what information is required to design, implement and monitor health policy. When Alkire and Santos claim that the MPI is policy relevant, what, precisely, do they have in mind? It has been suggested above that in South Africa there is a mountain of HIV/AIDS research available, some of which informs policy, and much of which probably does not. Constructing a measure that relates the HIV/AIDS contribution to the health/poverty nexus in South Africa at a national level, would be expensive, requiring as it would, something along the lines of the Mandela-HSRC study, but on a significantly expanded scale.[143]

The absence of this information need not, however, hamper continued implementation of the HIV/AIDS programme – although there are major

---

[143] Conducting surveys is complicated by the fact that in a setting in which the stigma associated with HIV/AIDS is intense, and possibly worsening (Maughan-Brown, 2009), few people voluntarily disclose their status, especially not to a survey enumerator.

disagreements about progress being made in the fight against the epidemic (Rehle and Shisana, 2009; Dorrington, 2009) enough is known to be getting on with in the meanwhile. The same, however, cannot be said of government's anti-poverty programmes. The glacial pace of poverty reduction (see Leibbrandt *et al*, 2010) is most emphatically not due to a reduction of the poverty problem to a simplistic concentration on income poverty. Although income or expenditure poverty are the most prominently and frequently measured aspects of this multi-dimensional blight in South Africa, as Noble *et al* show in their review of the literature, there is a long tradition of approaching poverty research from a multi-dimensional perspective (2006a, pp.9ff). Not only that, government has for years been critical of income (expenditure) poverty estimates, asserting forcibly that such measures overstate the extent of the problem because they ignore the 'social wage'. Acting on that belief, it has made substantial progress with regard to the provision of many of the basics of life. Nonetheless, it is also true that income poverty (closely linked to the failure of the labour market to cater for millions upon millions of mostly poorly qualified would-be workers), is severe and not showing much sign of diminishing.

In such a setting, the Alkire and Santos MPI for 2003 could do little other than offer some misguided consolation to a government that is way out of its depth in its attempts to address poverty – the 2008 MPI is better but by no means good enough to deserve the accolade 'policy relevant'. Education and health have to be dealt with adequately. Once that has been done, surveys big enough to allow useful things to be said at sub-national level will have to be found. Until the time that one comes along, is there anything to be gained from simulating income-specific prevalence rates?

Simulating prevalence rates

Although HIV/AIDS prevalence rates by income or expenditure category cannot be discovered by playing around with numbers, it should be possible to construct hypothetical distributions of PLWH among the categories of poor and non-poor in such a manner that some distributions are more plausible than others. The exercise carried out below does this in an attempt to show that prevalence rates among the non-poor have to pushed to implausibly high levels in order to ensure that the number of poor PLWH does not add a substantially to the total of those suffering multiple deprivations.

To kickstart the process, we begin with some 'facts' elicited from the ASSA 2008 model, and some from Statistics South Africa. These are brought together in Table 12 below. Numbers of HIV positive people for the year 2011 have been taken from the ASSA 2008 model. So too, has the total population figure.[144] The number of households (14 million) is guessed at, based on the figure in the 2009 General Household Survey (Statistical release P0318, 6 May 2010, p.95).[145] It requires just three sets of assumptions about the numbers involved to get the thing running – these are to be found in the grey-shaded rows of the table.

The first set contains two assumptions – the first of these is that someone whose HIV status is positive, and who is (income) poor, may be classified as deprived. Although ART makes it possible for many to lead 'normal' lives, inside them, the time bomb ticks – of 5.6 million PLWH in South Africa in 2011, 1.7 million or so were receiving ART. Among the 5.5 million PLWH, about 500 000 were AIDS sick (ASSA 2008). In Alkire's and Santos' terms, if there is one deprived person in a household in particular dimension (or indicator), then all household members are held to be deprived in that dimension as well (2010a, pp.13ff). In the case of HIV/AIDS, especially in poor households, this is not unreasonable. The second assumption is that everyone in the HIV/AIDS affected 'chronically poor' households is malnourished. Even Statistics South Africa, with its (possibly) more parsimonious food poverty line, had roughly one quarter of the population below it in 2006.

Following Tladi (2006), the population is divided into three groups: what I have called 'chronic poor'; the 'poor', and 'others', well aware of the fact that 'chronic' is a much-debated concept. In the exercise carried out below, the line marking off all of the poor from the non-poor is the lower bound of the poverty critical range demarcated by Leibbrandt et al, i.e., R515 per capita per month in 2008 prices – at that level, the poverty headcount rate is 54 per cent (2010, p.36). Chronic poverty is defined as subsisting on total expenditure below a food poverty line which stood at R313 per capita per month in 2008 prices (the Hoogeveen and Özler line of R211 per capita per month in 2000 prices).

Estimates of monthly per capita consumption at various headcount poverty rates for the year 2008 have been scaled from the 2008 cumulative distribution function in Figure 2.7 in the Leibbrandt et al paper (2010, p.41). Consumption levels are given in R/capita per month and expressed as well, as percentages of the R515 poverty

---

[144] The 2011 population estimate in the 2008 ASSA model is 50 840 588, while the number of people living with HIV/AIDS is 5 577 812.

[145] The number of single-person households, and hence the total number of households has grown very rapidly. It is not known whether or not this is real, or an artifact of the way in which sample frames have changed. For the beginnings of an exploration of this question, see Kerr and Wittenberg (2012).

line. It should be borne in mind that all those in a particular expenditure category have less to spend than the category upper bound.

The results of four simulations are presented in the table – the first two (simulations 1a and 1b) make use of a poverty line that slice offs the bottom two deciles of the population. Per capita monthly consumption among these folk would be less than R220 per month, or less than 43 per cent of the value of the poverty line.

Consumption is allowed to float upwards in Simulations 2-4 – only the biased estimates are given in the table. Simulation 2 makes use of the food poverty line of R313, which pushes the poverty headcount ratio to roughly 32 per cent (about 6-8 percentage points higher than Statistics South Africa's estimate of the rate at 'their' food poverty line). The headcount climbs from 10.2 to 16.3 million – people captured in that net are desperately poor.

In simulation 3, an additional 5.6 million folk consume more than R313 per month each, but less than R425. They take the poverty headcount rate up to 43 per cent, or between 61 and 83 per cent of the R515 poverty line. According to the Leibbrandt et al (2010) estimates for the year 2008, the consumption levels of more than half of the population were less than that amount – below the R515 line one thus finds 27.5 million people in simulation 4.

The second set of assumptions deals with mean household size. In general, poorer households tend to have more members than wealthier ones. What happens among the very poor is a complicated story. For the purposes of the present exercise, I am assuming that among them, resources are so scarce that households cannot support more than a few members. In simulation 1, the mean number of household members in 'other' households has been pegged at 4.1. This fixes mean household size among the 'chronically poor' in the bottom two deciles of the population at 2.5 persons. Simulation 2 pushes mean household size in non-poor households to 4.0; simulation 3 to 3.9 and simulation 4 to 3.8. This sees the corresponding household mean household size among all poor households rise to 3.5 persons. If the data set used by Leibbrandt *et al* were to hand, these parameters could be fixed with precision. As it is though, the assumptions used are conservative – the greater the household size among the poor, the greater the number suffering multiple deprivation when a member of the household is diagnosed as HIV positive.

It appears to be reasonably well established that among the very poor, HIV prevalence rates are lower than they are among the better off. The third set of assumptions attempt to deal with what may be called this 'bias'. In Simulations 1a and 1b, the results in the 'a' column are based on the assumption that HIV/AIDS is distributed randomly throughout the population. With a large population, we would expect the number of people living with HIV/AIDS (PLWH) to be evenly distributed, if this neutral assumption held true. In the 'b' simulation, it is assumed that for every 100 instances of PLWH among the 'chronically poor', there are 120 such people among the 'others'. As consumption levels rise, the bias rate is assumed to rise as well, reaching 35 per cent among the 7.8 million 'poor' households.

Table 12 Simulated distributions of PLWH in poor households

	Chronically poor			Poor	
Simulation	1a	1b	2	3	4
Poverty headcount rate (%)	20	20	32	43	54
Poor (millions)	10.2	10.2	16.3	21.9	27.5
Others (millions)	40.7	40.7	34.6	29.0	23.4
Per capita consumption					
Less than R/month in 2008 prices	220	220	313	425	515
As % of R515/month poverty line	43	43	61	83	100
Mean household size					
Poor households	2.5	2.5	3.0	3.3	3.5
Other households	4.1	4.1	4.0	3.9	3.8
Nos. of households (millions)					
Poor households	4.1	4.1	5.4	6.6	7.8
Other households	9.9	9.9	8.6	7.4	6.2
Bias (%)	Neutral	20	25	30	35
Distribution of PLWH among households (millions)					
In poor households	1.1	0.2	0.8	1.4	2.1
In other households	4.5	5.4	4.7	4.1	3.5
Implied prevalence rate (%)					
In poor households	11.0	2.2	5.1	6.6	7.7
In other households	11.0	13.2	13.7	14.3	14.8
Max no. suffering multiple deprivation in poor households (millions)	2.8	0.6	2.5	(4.8)	(7.4)

And that, really is all there is to it – the last row of the table contains the results. These represent the maximum numbers that would have to be added to the total numbers of MPI poor in both the 2003 and 2008 MPIs.

If the headcount poverty rate is 20 per cent, then under the neutral assumption (Simulation 1a) 2.8 million more people could have joined the ranks of those suffering multiple deprivation. In Simulation 1b, the assumed bias of 20 per cent causes the number of PLWH to fall to 200 000, and thus the number suffering multiple-deprivation poverty to drop to 0.6 million. Expressed in prevalence rate terms, this suggests that with a national rate of 11 per cent, the rate for those in the bottom two deciles is a mere 2.2 per cent, while that for the remainder of the population (40.7 million people) is 13.2 per cent. The latter figure is plausible, but the implied prevalence rate of 2.2 per cent for the chronically poor surely cannot be.

At the food poverty line, the assumptions used yield 800 000 PLWH, a prevalence rate of 5.1 per cent and 2.5 million people in 5.4 million households suffering multiple deprivation. When the poverty line R515 per capita per month is reached, the number of PLWH has climbed to 2.1 million, while the prevalence rate has reached 7.7 per cent.

Among the chronically poor, the estimates of the numbers experiencing multiple deprivation have to be reduced by the extent to which Alkire and her co-workers have managed to pick up mortality and malnourishment in the surveys they used. The numbers involved in the 2003 MPI are trivial, in the 2008 MPI less so. Between them, mortality and malnutrition account for more than half of total deprivation in that year (see Figure 2 above). The mortality figures are, however, for children under the age of five years (Alkire and Santos, 2010a, p.15). According to the 2008 ASSA model, among the 5.6 million PLWH, there are only[146] 190 000 under-fives. Prime cause of death among that age cohort (38 000 infants and 12 000 1-4 year-olds) is not AIDS. How big the adjustments should be is impossible to determine with any precision – my sense is that it would not be very big.

Not all of the 2.3 million poor people (4.8 - 2.5) in expenditure category R313-425 who live in households in which at least one person is HIV positive, will necessarily suffer multiple deprivation, as defined above. Nor indeed, will the 2.6 million (7.4 -

---

[146] The record of deaths (for the year 2009) is from Statistical release P0309.3, 30 November 2011, p.60. Writing a sentence that contains the phrase 'only 190 000 children are HIV positive' makes one feel more than just a little queasy. In the UK in 2010, there were estimated to be a total of 91 500 PLWH. Downloaded from the National AIDS Trust (NAT) website, http://www.nat.org.uk/HIV-Facts/Statistics/Latest-UK-Statistics.aspx, 22 February 2012. The UK's population is quite a lot bigger than South Africa's.

4.8) in expenditure category R425-515. Some downward adjustment of these numbers may be necessary, depending on what other deprivations those below the R515 poverty line experience. If, as has been argued above, nearly all poor people suffer deprivation as a result of the poor quality of the education they receive, and the poor quality of the health services available to them, the downward adjustment may not be very large.

The outcome of this exercise is the sense it gives of the possible magnitude of the omission of nearly all of the PLWH from the Alkire *et al* estimates of both the 2003 and the 2008 MPIs. The number of MPI poor to be added (if that number could be determined, as opposed to merely being simulated), looks as though it could at least double the 6.6 million claimed by the 2008 MPI to be suffering multi-dimensional poverty.

Section 6 The end, apart from power struggles & the persistence of poverty

South Africa is involved in a number of battles to undo the heritage of its colonial past (apartheid, bastard offspring of the standard colonial practice of segregation, could, in part, be viewed as a ruthless attempt to stall the process of decolonisation until what many still regard as the 'colonisers', were reasonably sure of being able to live in the style which they believed was their due). The apartheid heritage is particularly acute in the areas of health and education.[147] Poverty estimates, it hardly need be said, are intensely political. Anyone who enters the poverty and inequality arena has a duty to ensure that when they do, they are not peddling rubbish. If, despite being rubbish, it smells complimentary to the ANC, especially if it carries the trademark 'international scholars' and 'Oxford University', then one can be sure that sooner or later, some clown will try to get political mileage out of it, a sport that may have deleterious consequences for anti-poverty policy design.

Pondering on the insistence of Alkire and her colleagues of imbuing MPIs with the essence of 'capabilities', it seems to me that if many of them are non-measurable, or extremely difficult to tie tightly to the proxies used to detect them, then the continued attempt to 'measure' them is quixotic.[148] Easing up on the quest for the Holy Grail need not be cause for alarm – conceptually, the capabilities approach is undeniably powerful. It is a bit like love though, we know that it is supremely important – we have no need of an index to tell us so. In the section of the paper on critiques of the MPI, we saw that one of the mechanisms by which the MPI 'dimensions' were selected, is 'theory', "... as in the many philosophical or

---

[147] By comparison, making good the deficit in infrastructure is child's play – award a contract to a private sector firm or a giant state-owned enterprise, and hey presto, physical assets appear. Riddled as it is with corruption, especially among those adjudicating tender processes, and their favoured contractors, the cost of doing business is often vastly inflated South Africa. Generally, however, when it comes to physical assets, if quality control is strict, the private sector delivers.

[148] Wikipedia says that quixotic is: "impracticality in pursuit of ideals, especially those ideals manifested by rash, lofty and romantic ideas" – is the insistence on the measurability of capabilities inspired by some 'lofty' ideal? If so, then laying at the feet of Amartya Sen, part of the blame for the poor performance of the MPI in South Africa and possibly elsewhere, along with the seemingly overblown ambitions its creators have for it, may be justified. Then again, maybe not, for as was noted above, Sen has apparently spoken out against the possibility of measuring capabilities – recall here the passage from Silva-Leander (2011, p.1) cited above, to the effect that: "... several proponents [among them, Sen himself] of the capability approach have suggested that, for the sake of measurement, practitioners may have to "be content with achievements, instead of capabilities" Details of the Sen documents referred to may be found in the Silva-Leander paper.

psychological accounts of basic needs, universal values, human rights, and so on" (Alkire and Santos, 2010a, p.12). Trying via that route to locate the selection process in a 'capabilities' framework, while coping with the severe data constraints that caused them to generate such rubbish for South Africa the first time around, seems like pure indulgence. It is possible to construct an MPI with no recourse whatsoever to mumbo-jumbo about capabilities – it is equally possible for others to engage critically with the index without reference to 'capabilities'. So, let us look back on what has been found, pretending that the word has never been uttered.

If multiple deprivation were the fate of some small proportion of the population, (as suggested by the 2003 MPI), it would have implied that anti-poverty measures had largely been successful. In that case, the policy message sent out by the MPI would presumably have been that government should devote its energy, Rawlsian style, to finding the 3.1 per cent of the population or maybe more) the MPI said was suffering multiple deprivation? Naturally, their immediate suffering should be addressed with all possible speed.

That raises the question of where the responsibility for doing so should lie. There is no simple answer to this – part of the task should be carried out by competent local authorities, and part by the institutions of national government. In principle, municipalities or local authorities should be able to identify and provide certain services (housing, utilities, and schooling) to take care of those suffering acute multi-dimensional poverty. Social grants provided through national-level institutions should alleviate income poverty – local authorities could help to expedite claims.

It has not worked this way in practice. The MPI (even the 2008 version), understates the extent of deprivation, a problem of such magnitude as would even have challenged even the best bureaucracy. First of all, the massive gap in South Africa's social protection system, the absence of social grants for the working age poor, be they employed, unemployed or not economically active, serves to keep millions in poverty, whether they are recipients of other elements of the 'social wage' or not.

In the second place, municipalities and local authorities have not managed their share of the job successfully (witness the hundreds of demonstrations about poor service delivery).[149] This does not demonstrate that the principle of devolution is

---

[149] Among the many things municipalities failed to manage successfully was the system of grants for the indigent. The job should never have been given to them in the first place.

wrong, rather, it shows flaws in both policy design, and implementation, and above all, the weakness (incompetence and corruption) of the civil service.[150]

In the face of multiple government failures, of such a magnitude, what has the MPI to offer? At one point in their story, Alkire and Santos note that they:

> "… believe that a multidimensional measure such as the MPI constitutes a powerful and necessary instrument to evaluate poverty but is not sufficient (*sic*); it could usefully be complemented by income measures." (Alkire and Santos, 2010a, p.44)

In the South African case, neither the 2003 MPI nor its 2008 replacement is powerful or necessary. If 'complementing the 2008 MPI with income measures' means more of the same trivia that was criticised in the discussion about the Table 2 above, then it will not help – what is required is more and better data.

When a claim is made that a particular measuring instrument is 'policy relevant', it is not unreasonable to require of those making the claim that they demonstrate the instrument's ability to perform in ways that are policy relevant. If by policy relevant, the compilers of an index like the MPI were to mean that it could be used to monitor some existing policy to which government is already committed, such as, for example, some (but not all) of the Millennium Development Goals, then the task

---

[150] At the time of writing this note (March 2012), the country was in political uproar caused by the assumption of control by the National Treasury of delinquent departments in three provinces, Gauteng, the Free State and Limpopo. Exercising the constitutional right of central government to intervene when provincial (and local) government fails, Treasury is having to pick up the pieces of the disaster caused by gross incompetence and corruption. At the point of final incidence, the victims are schoolchildren who start the school year without books; new schools standing empty for want of desks; classes with no teachers because of deployment problems, and more immediately threateningly, hospital patients who cannot be fed because suppliers either have not been paid or are not assured of payment. The supplier problem goes way beyond school books and food, reaching into the myriad items needed, some critically, to keep services afloat. There are dozens of newspaper articles dealing with the issues – here is a small sample: Piet Rampedi, "Fraudulent tenders milk Limpopo treasury", (*Sunday Independent*) *Independent-on-line*, 29 January 2012; Paul Hoffman, "Disregard for constitution led to financial crisis in Limpopo", *Business Day*, 27 January 2012; Lynley Donnelly, "Province in crisis: Battle lines drawn in Limpopo", *Mail & Guardian*, 20 January 2012; The Editorial, "Power, patronage and the provinces", *Mail & Guardian*, 9 December 2011; Lynley Donnelly, "No more cash for provinces", *Mail & Guardian*, 9 December 2011; Bekezela Phakathi. "Use court orders on hospital suppliers — Sama: Medical association says government should approach courts to interdict suppliers and avoid patient care being compromised", *Business Day*, 27 January 2012.

of showing that it can do what is required would be a relatively simple one – provided that the instrument is fed a steady diet of data from a suitably designed survey, out would pop the relevant results. These could easily be checked for adequacy.

Alkire and Santos are, however, more ambitious than that – in the abstract of their 2010a paper it is asserted that:

> "This tool could be used to target the poorest, track the Millennium Development Goals, and design policies that directly address the interlocking deprivations poor people experience."[151]

In principle, the MPI is capable of informing government about the numbers of 'multi-dimensionally poor' (in the case of the 2003 South African MPI, within a range whose upper limit was unknown); their approximate location (province or state – but not at present in the South African case); the dominant forms of deprivation they suffer, and a couple of the other characteristics they share, all by membership of one goup of folk or another.

The claim that 'tool could be used to target the poorest' surely cannot be intended to mean that the instrument in its existing form can contribute directly to the task of bringing relief to the unfortunates who most urgently need it.[152] If that were the intended meaning, then it almost certainly overstates the MPI's usefulness. To achieve such a goal, the instrument would have to be used in conjunction with other, more precise tools (as they themselves have pointed out), tools capable, for example, of telling policymakers where the potential beneficiaries are located, how many there are of them, of what age, sex and a whole range of other characteristics. Not only that, it would have also be able to do so regularly, with fresh data (recall here, the Indian BPL census).

Notwithstanding the express hopes of Alkire *et al* that data will improve, it is difficult to believe that surveys of appropriate size will be conducted at the required intervals (regularly and frequently) in the near future, especially not in countries with significant poverty problems.

---

[151] As was noted in Section 2 of the present paper, it is claimed that the MPI can help to: "Target the poorest groups and beneficiaries of conditional cash transfers, district interventions or public programmes."

[152] Even a very large survey like South Africa's 2007 Community Survey (with a sample of 270 000 households) cannot pinpoint potential beneficiaries of whatever programmes have been dreamed up to improve their conditions of existence.

Every so often, countries committed to achieving the MDGs have to compile a progress report. In the Acknowledgements page of South Africa's 2010 report (put together by Statistics South Africa), the Statistician-General says that:

> "In an endeavour to make the MDGs relevant to South Africa, a number of indicators were domesticated and a total of 95 indicators were addressed to address (*sic*) the eight MDG goals." (Stats SA, 2011a, p.2)

Leave aside for a moment, the fact that these 95 indicators cannot tell us how many people suffer acute multi-dimensional poverty, and then compare the amount of information they do convey with that offered by the MPI (which, according to Alkire and Santos, can track some of the MDGs). The very least one may expect from a modest source of information like the MPI is that it agree, roughly, with the figures provided by the individual countries. Yet as has been shown in Section 3 of the present paper, there are substantial differences between the Statistics South Africa income poverty estimates, and those made by Alkire and Santos. Either, or possibly both sets of estimates could be wrong. If MPIs are going to continue to be produced, it were a good idea if that were done in collaboration with national statistics authorities in the countries concerned. Then, at least, readers would be spared the problem of trying to decide which, if any, of the figures to trust (sadly, not all national statistics agencies are trustworthy).

Section 3 of the paper also directs our attention to the 'failure' of Alkire and Santos to refer to the work of another University of Oxford group in the business of measuring multiple deprivation. The impression this creates is one of overwhelming single-mindedness in the pursuit of a composite index that tells us, as the old aphorism (suitably paraphrased) has it, almost everything we ever wanted to know about poverty but were afraid to ask. Examining one of the more prominent instruments that play tunes something like those croaked out by the MPI – the Noble *et al* Index of Multiple Deprivation (which actually is used in policy formation) – we discover that these folk, although not brave (foolhardy?) enough to essay an estimate of poverty levels, look to have chosen a better indicator for that hard-to-measure domain or dimension, health. And thereby hangs a tale.

In order to construct a 'respectable' international comparative series of MPIs, it looks as though Alkire and Santos felt a need to populate their league table with results from as many countries as possible. Casting the net widely places a tight constraint on the number of indicator variables that can be used. Noble *et al* do not face such a severe constraint. This brings to mind an engineering metaphor, Euler's Slenderness Ratio, an early attempt to bring some predictability to the likelihood of a column collapsing, an event that can occur without warning, and at lower load levels than the strength in compression of the material in question would suggest.

Something similar ought to be estimated for the MPIs as well – be their axiomatic structure never so rigorous,[153] in the final analysis, if that structure cannot bear the load imposed upon it, the edifice collapses. As is shown in the sections of the present paper on education and health (3 and 4), the 2003 MPI collapsed in fairly spectacular fashion. In short, although the mathematics of the MPI look to be the very last word in rigour, that attribute provides little protection against the possibility that the indicators chosen to make up the MPI may not do what they are supposed to.[154] Nor, indeed does it offer any guarantee that the surveys on which particular MPIs estimates rest, are suitable for the job they are required to do (the WHS used to estimate South Africa's 2003 MPI was wholly unsuitable).

Despite the resources, financial, intellectual, physical and political, that have been thrown at the task of creating the MPI, it fails to detect a major, long-standing and continuing crisis in education, manifest in the poor quality of educational outcomes. The crisis is multi-dimensional: the inability of malnourished pupils from impoverished households to learn; the inability, for a variety of reasons, of teachers to teach; the incompetence of an army of civil servants to ensure that a proper, safe learning environment exists, to name but three elements of it. Alkire and Santos recognise that the inability of their chosen indicators to measure 'quality' is a drawback – in South Africa's case, the drawback is as large as an elephant's foreskin.[155] Their risible '3.2 per cent' (see Table 3 above) was an insult to researchers who toiled long and hard to produce the evidence that has persuaded even blindly sycophantic ANC functionaries that solving the education crisis is imperative.

---

[153] Alkire and Santos assure us that: "Axiomatically [the MPI's] mathematical structure ... satisfies a number of properties that are widely regarded as desirable in the poverty measurement literature." (2010a, p.65). Obviously, a great deal of effort has been expended to provide the MPI with a good launch pad. This is evident in many places – the 2009 Alkire and Foster paper, for example. When, however, the available data are so poor as to prevent sensible results from being generated, boasting about how many axioms the poverty index complies with is an exercise in futility.

[154] In the 2010 HDR (which presents the work of Alkire *et al*) it is acknowledged that: "the MPI has some drawbacks, due mainly to data constraints. First, the indicators include both outputs (such as years of schooling) and inputs (such as cooking fuel) as well as one stock indicator (child mortality, which could reflect a death that was recent or long ago), because flow data are not available for all dimensions. Second, the health data are relatively weak or have poor coverage, especially for nutrition, though the patterns that emerge are plausible and familiar." (UNDP, 2010, p.99)

[155] According to Table 4.09, "Quality of primary education", in the *Global Competitiveness Report 2011–2012* (Schwab and Sala-i-Martin, 2011, p.438), South Africa was ranked at position 127 out of 142 countries – Zimbabwe was 68th.

Many will be familiar with the tart comment in Oscar Wilde's play *The Importance of Being Earnest* aimed at the chief protagonist: "To lose one parent, Mr Worthing, may be regarded as a misfortune; to lose two looks like carelessness." In Mr Worthing's case, the pronouncement was an injustice – accusing Alkire and Santos of carelessness would not be. Because of the indicators they have chosen (have been obliged to choose?), they 'lose' the multiple epidemics that beset South Africa's population. Because of the indicators they have not chosen, and the analysis they have not conducted, they manage to 'lose' the profound crisis in South Africa's health services.

In the face of the catastrophe that has engulfed the already fragile health system in South Africa, the two indicators selected by Alkire and Santos to measure the health dimension look more than just a little inadequate. Once chosen, complete reliance (i.e., a failure to subject the indicators to a reality check) on the limited survey data available, leads to a predictable outcome. Deserving though Alkire and Santos are of criticism, it has to be acknowledged that health is the very devil of an area in which to have to work. The frustrating search for estimates of the burden on the poor of the HIV/AIDS and TB epidemics conducted above is proof, if any were wanted, of that. Of course it is difficult to obtain reliable numbers on HIV/AIDS. That, however, is no excuse for not facing up to the question of when it is inappropriate to include a country in an international comparative study. If the chosen health indicators in a particular country are not up to scratch, and if data constraints are such that no suitable alternatives can be found, the case for omission is strong. At very least, if a fragile result is to be published, it should be richly larded with health warnings (pardon the mixed metaphor) – there does not appear to be any indication in the 2010 HDR, for example, that the value given for the South African MPI should be treated as a lower bound.

Apart from the AIDS/HIV and TB plagues, morbidity and mortality are likely to be a greater among the poor than the well-off. Writing about the advanced countries of the OECD (the USA excepted), most of which have universal health care, Joumard *et al* observe that:

> "Rather than the health care system, socio-economic factors are important in shaping inequalities in health status. Many studies conclude that those with a lower income, less education or employment in a less prestigious occupation tend to have a higher prevalence of illness and die at a younger age." (2011, p.11)

While the conclusions about socio-economic status are almost certainly true for South Africa, the opening statement needs to be qualified – in South Africa (and elsewhere) the 'inverse care law' – the "availability of good medical care tends to vary inversely with the need for the population served." (Hart, 1971) operates. The poor in South Africa are thus doubly afflicted – not only is low socio-economic status associated with greater morbidity, the likelihood of receiving quality health care also falls as one descends the income ladder.

Starting from a standpoint which regarded the 2003 MPI for South Africa created by Alkire and Santos with more than a little suspicion (it simply did not accord with my knowledge and experience of the country), the trawl through the literature suggests to me that the project of performing international comparisons using the 'mashup' MPI is probably a waste of time and money (marginal cost > marginal benefit?). The 2008 MPI, although a bit more plausible, does little to change that perception. Countries sufficiently well-endowed to conduct their own analyses probably have little need of it, except possibly as an instrument of political propaganda, while countries not so blessed have need of far more comprehensive analyses, while at the same time suffering from a dearth of survey data of the sort required to make the MPI dream come true. This is not to say that an AF-type analysis made using adequate data (and reality checks) are necessarily useless – rather it is to suggest that international league tables are silly.[156]

Similarly we know that socio-economic status is associated with all manner of bads (there are some indiscriminate exceptions, like HIV). As everybody keeps insisting, to discover the extent of those bads, what needs to be heard is the voice of the poor – recall that OPHI, the institution headed by Alkire has as its *raison d'être* the goal of building "…a multidimensional economic framework for reducing poverty grounded in people's experiences and values… ". Where the silence is most deafening, it will invariably be found that issues of governance are involved – that, and the distribution of power. The likelihood of 'people's experiences and values' finding their way into the MPI for South Africa (and elsewhere) in a meaningful way (a handful of consultations doth not 'ground' an MPI) is remote. Not only is the MPI unlikely to empower the poor – its effect may well be the opposite, as Smith and Joumard *et al* warn.[157]

---

[156] If too much noise were made about capabilities and the HDI, one may feel tempted to view the international array of these indices as a silliness as well. Crude as it is, however, the use of life expectancy as an indicator did at least enable South Africa's HDI to pick up the HIV/AIDS epidemic.

[157] Indices like the Human Development Index (HDI), the Multi-dimensional Poverty Index (MPI), the Gender Inequality Index (GII), and several others, may well be able to exert some leverage on policy, without empowering the poor. Trying to measure this effect would be a devil of a job. It may be possible to discover under what conditions governments become receptive to bad news about their (relative) performance. Once again though, finding out would be difficult.

An eminent South African sociologist, Eddie Webster, once quipped at a seminar that: "knowledge isn't power – power is power". The exercise of power is central to the persistence of poverty and inequality. They are not natural phenomena, something caused by crop failure or the like – rather, they are reproduced through the repeated exercise of human agency and power within structures and institutions, usually created by others. In a dynamic world, these structures and institutions evolve as changes in the balance of forces acting on them take place. In seeking to understand the limits of agency, we ignore structure and the way in which it changes or persists, at our peril – the mere act of placing information in the public domain, especially information that can be challenged and swept aside by the powerful, can only change the world under certain, special circumstances.

The UNDP, by its very nature, is poorly placed to help effect such changes. It is tightly constrained in what it may say about conditions in member countries of the UN – imagine the furore if the UNDP told a few home truths like: 'the reason why poverty and inequality in your country are still so high is that your leader is a murderous, corrupt, thieving scumbag, who has been able to maintain his position only by means of a combination of patronage and violent repression'.

South Africa could not now be judged so harshly. It would not, however, be too far wide of the mark to observe that it is a combination of corruption and incompetence, coupled with an inability to reverse the trend towards greater inequality, a trend reinforced by the malevolent workings of the labour market (probably not much assisted by the trades union's struggles for decent conditions of existence), that sees the absolute number of poor rising, swamping the state's best efforts to secure the most basic conditions of existence for possibly half of the population, or at least some significant minority of it. What possible contribution can the MPI make to fixing this mess?

References

Aglietta, Michel; Sabina Alkire; François Bourguignon; Andrew E. Clark; Angus Deaton and Claudia Senik. *Measure for Measure: How Well do We Measure Development?*, Proceedings of the 8th AFD/EUDN Conference, held in Paris December 2010, organised by the Agence Française de Développement (AFD) and the European Development Research Network (EUDN), Paris, 2011. Referred to as Aglietta *et al*, 2011.

Alkire, Sabina and Suman Seth. "Measuring Multidimensional Poverty in India: A New Proposal", Oxford Poverty & Human Development Initiative (OPHI) Working Paper No. 15, September 2008 [rev. May 2009]. Referred to as Alkire and Seth, 2008.

Alkire, Sabina, and James Foster. "Counting and Multidimensional Poverty Measurement", Oxford Poverty & Human Development Initiative (OPHI) Working Paper No. 7, 2009.

Alkire, Sabina. "Human Development: Definitions, Critiques, and Related Concepts: Background paper for the 2010 Human Development Report", Oxford Poverty & Human Development Initiative (OPHI) Working Paper No. 36, May 2010.

Alkire, Sabina, and James Foster. "Designing the Inequality-Adjusted Human Development Index (HDI)", Oxford Poverty & Human Development Initiative (OPHI) Working Paper No. 37, July 2010.

Alkire, Sabina, and Maria Emma Santos. "Acute Multidimensional Poverty: A New Index for Developing Countries", Oxford Poverty & Human Development Initiative (OPHI) Working Paper No. 38, July 2010a.

Alkire, Sabina, and Maria Emma Santos. *South Africa Country Briefing*, Oxford Poverty & Human Development Initiative (OPHI) Multidimensional Poverty Index Country Briefing Series, 2010b. Available at: www.ophi.org.uk/policy/multidimensional-poverty-index/mpi-country-briefings/.

Alkire, Sabina; Jose Manuel Roche; Maria Emma Santos and Suman Seth. *South Africa Country Briefing*. Oxford Poverty & Human Development Initiative (OPHI) Multidimensional Poverty Index Country Briefing Series. Available at: www.ophi.org.uk/policy/multidimensional-poverty-index/mpi-country-briefings/. Referred to as Alkire *et al*, 2011.

Alkire, Sabina and Foster, James. "Counting and multidimensional poverty measurement", *Journal of Public Economics*, Vol. 95, Issues 7-8, August 2011, pp.476-487.

Alkire, Sabina and James Foster. "Counting and Multidimensional Poverty Measurement", OPHI Working Paper 7, Oxford Poverty and Human Development Initiative, Oxford, UK. Cited in UNDP, 2010, p.125.

Alkire, Sabina. "Multidimensional Poverty and its Discontents", pp.55-90 in Aglietta *et al*, 2011. Referred to as Alkire, 2011.

Alkire, Sabina, and James Foster. "Understandings and Misunderstandings of Multidimensional Poverty Measurement", Oxford Poverty & Human Development Initiative (OPHI) Working Paper No. 43, May 2011.

Alkire, Sabina; James Foster, and Maria Emma Santos. "Where Did Identification Go?", Oxford Poverty & Human Development Initiative (OPHI) Working Paper No. 43b, September 2011.

Anand, P; G Hunter, and R Smith. "Capabilities and well-being: evidence based on the Sen-Nussbaum approach to welfare", *Social Indicators Research*, 2005, Vol. 74, Issue 9-55.

Anand, P. "Capabilities and health", *Journal of Medical Ethics*, 2005; Vol. 31, pp.299–303.

Anand, Paul; Graham Hunter; Ian Carter; Keith Dowding; Francesco Guala, and Martin van Hees. "The Measurement of Capabilities", unpublished paper, The Open University, 2007.

Anand, Paul; Santos, Cristina and Smith, Ron. "The measurement of capabilities", in Basu, Kaushik and Ravi Kanbur (eds), *Arguments for a Better World: Essays in Honour of Amartya Sen: Volume I: Ethics, Welfare, and Measurement*, Oxford: Oxford University Press, pp. 283–310, 2009 (electronic version).

Babita, Miriam; Berk Özler; Nozipho Shabalala, and Harry Thema. "Changes in Poverty and Inequality in South Africa: 1995-2000", Unpublished manuscript, Statistics South Africa, 2003. Cited in Hoogeveen and Özler, 2005.

Barnett, T, and A Whiteside. *AIDS in the Twenty-First Century*, London: Palgrave Macmillan, 2006.

Bateman, Chris. "Health Services Battle as KZN's Budget Implodes", *South African Medical Journal*, February 2009a, Vol. 99, No. 2, pp.76-79.

Bateman, Chris. "No pay, no cure – can our hospitals be salvaged?", *South African Medical Journal*, May 2009b, Vol. 99, No. 5, pp.288-292.

Basarir, Hasan. "Poor, Multidimensionally Speaking: Evidence from South Africa", *Journal of African Economies*, Vol. 20, No. 3, pp.463–504, doi:10.1093/jae/ejr001 online date 11 March 2011.

Benatar, Solomon R. "Health Care Reform and the Crisis of HIV and AIDS in South Africa", *New England Journal of Medicine*, July 2004, Vol. 351, pp.81-92.

Bennett, Sarah. "Under the surface: a critique of the HSRC HIV/AIDS survey", Commentary by ASSA AIDS Committee, May 2003. Downloaded on 30 November 2011 from http://www.eldis.org/vfile/upload/1/document/0708/DOC12034.pdf

Bergman, Manfred Max; Zinette Bergman and Sarah Gravett. "The development and application of the Explanatory Model of School Dysfunctions", *South African Journal of Education*, 2011, Vol. 31, pp.461-474.

Berthoud, Richard; Mark Bryan, and Elena Bardasi. "The dynamics of deprivation: the relationship between income and material deprivation over time," Department for Work and Pensions [UK], Families and Children Strategic Analysis Programme, Research Report No 219, 2004.

Bhorat, Haroon and Ravi Kanbur (eds). *Poverty and Policy in Post-Apartheid South Africa*, Cape Town: HSRC, 2006.

Bjorkman, Hakan (NHDR Facilitator). "NHDR [National Human Development Report] Network Consolidated Answer to Request from UNDP Bulgaria on GDP component in municipal HDI, 19 February 2000. Referred to as Bjorkman, 2000.

Bloch, Graeme. *The Toxic Mix: What's wrong with South Africa's schools and how to fix it*, Cape Town: Tafelberg Publishers, 2009.

Bourguignon, F, and S Chakravarty. "The Measurement of Multidimensional Poverty." *Journal of Economic Inequality*, 2003, Vol. 1, No. 1, pp.25–49. Cited in UNDP, 2010, p.125.

Bradshaw, Debbie ; Michelle Schneider; Rob Dorrington; David E Bourne, and Ria Laubscher. "South African Cause-Of-Death Profile in Transition – 1996 and Future Trends", *South African Medical Journal*, August 2002, Vol. 92, No. 8, pp.618-623.

Bradshaw, D, and R Dorrington. "Child mortality in South Africa – we have lost touch", *South African Medical Journal*, 2007; Vol. 97, No. 8, pp.582-583.

Brandolini, A, and G D'Alessio. "Measuring Well-Being in the Functioning Space", in Chiappero-Martinetti, E (ed), *Debating Global Society: Reach and Limits of the Capability Approach*, Milan, Italy: Feltrinelli Foundation, 2009. Cited in UNDP, 2010, p.125.

Bray, Rachel; Imke Gooskens; Lauren Kahn; Sue Moses, and Jeremy Seekings. *Growing up in the new South Africa, Childhood and Adolescence in Post-Apartheid Cape Town*, Cape Town: HSRC Press, 2010.

Brewer, Mike, and Robert Joyce. *Child and Working-Age Poverty from 2010 to 2013*, London: Institute for Fiscal Studies, IFS Briefing Note 115, December 2010.

Burns, Justine and Malcolm Keswell. "Inheriting the Future: Intergenerational Persistence of Educational status in KwaZulu-Natal, South Africa", SALDRU Working Paper 71, Southern African Labour and Development Research Unit, University of Cape Town, November 2011.

Casale, Marisa, and Alan Whiteside. "The Impact of HIV/AIDS on Poverty, Inequality and Economic Growth", IDRC Working Papers on Globalization, Growth and Poverty, Working Paper No. 3, March 2006.

Chen, Shaohua and Martin Ravallion. "The Developing World Is Poorer Than We Thought, But No Less Successful in the Fight against Poverty", The World Bank Development Research Group, Policy Research Working Paper 4703, August 2009 version.

Clark, David A. "The Capability Approach: Its Development, Critiques and Recent Advances", Global Poverty Research Group (an Economic & Research Council Research Group), GPRG-WPS-032, 2005?

Coovadia, Hoosen; Rachel Jewkes; Peter Barron; David Sanders, and Diane McIntyre. *Health in South Africa 1. The health and health system of South Africa: historical roots of current public health challenges*, http://www.thelancet.com published online August 25, 2009.

Craig, Gary; Tania Burchardt and David Gordon (eds). *Social Justice and Public Policy: Seeking fairness in diverse societies*, Bristol: The Policy Press, 2008.

Crawford, Rowena; Carl Emmerson, and Gemma Tetlow. *A Survey of Public Spending in the UK*, IFS Briefing Note BN 42, Institute for Fiscal Studies, September 2009.

Crisp, Nicholas. "South Africa needs more doctors and dentists", (editorial), *South African Medical Journal*, August 2011, Vol. 101, No. 8, pp.517-518.

de Paoli, Marina Manuela; Arne Backer Grønningsæter, and Elizabeth Mills. *HIV/AIDS, the disability grant and ARV adherence: Summary report*, Fafo Report 2010:28, Fafo Institute for Labour and Social Research, Oslo/Cape Town, August 2010.

Department of Basic Education. *Action Plan to 2014: Towards the Realisation of Schooling 2025*, Notice 752 of 2010, Government Gazette No. 33434, 2 August 2010.

Department of Basic Education. *Macro Indicator Trends in Schooling: Summary Report 2011*, Pretoria, 2011.

Department of Health. *South Africa: Demographic and Health Survey 2003*, Pretoria: Department of Health, 2007. Referred to as DoH, 2007.

Department of Health. Budget Speech of Honourable Dr A Motsoaledi, MP, Minister of Health, delivered to the National Assembly, Parliament of the Republic Of South Africa on

30 June 2009, Downloaded from http://www.pmg.org.za/briefing/20090630-health-ministers-budget-speech 20 November 2011. Referred to as DoH, 2009.

Department of Health. *National Antenatal Sentinel HIV and Syphilis Prevalence Survey in South Africa, 2009*, Pretoria: Department of Health, 2010.

Department of Health. *Human Resources for Health, South Africa 2030: Draft HR Strategy for the Health Sector: 2012/13 – 2016/17, Consultation Document V5*, 2009, Pretoria: Department of Health, August 2011.

Department for Work and Pensions, and Department for Education. *A New Approach to Child Poverty: Tackling the Causes of Disadvantage and Transforming Families' Lives*, Cm 8061, April 2011. Referred to as DfWP and DfE, 2011.

Development Bank of Southern Africa. Education Roadmap: Focus on schooling system, November 2008. DBSA roadmap process. PowerPoint presentation, downloaded 30 November 2010, from http://www.dbsa.org/Research/Education%20Roadmap/A%2010%20point%20plan%20for%20education.pdf. Referred to as DBSA, 2008.

Dibben, C; I. Atherton; M Cox; V Watson; M Ryan, and M Sutton. Investigating the impact of changing the weights that underpin the Index of Multiple Deprivation 2004, Department for Communities and Local Government, London, 2007.

Dorrington, Rob. "Does the 2008 HSRC survey indicate a turning tide of HIV prevalence in children, teenagers and the youth?", *South African Medical Journal*, September 2009, Vol. 99, No. 9, pp.631-633.

Elbers, Chris; Tomoki Fujii; Peter Lanjouw; Berk Özler; and Wesley Yin. "Poverty Alleviation through Geographic Targeting: How Much Does Disaggregation Help?", World Bank Policy Research Working Paper 3419, October 2004.

Fleisch, Braam. *Primary Education in Crisis: Why South African schoolchildren underachieve in reading and mathematics*, Cape Town: Juta, 2008.

Fischer, Andrew M. "Towards Genuine Universalism within Contemporary Development Policy", *IDS Bulletin*, January 2010, Vol. 41 No. 1, pp.36-44.

Foster, James; Joel Greer and Erik Thorbecke. "A class of decomposable poverty measures", *Econometrica*, Vol. 52, 1984, pp.761–765.

Freije, Samuel. "JOBS – Addressing the Issue of Youth Unemployment: Issues and the Causes", World Development Report Team, World Bank, March 2012. See http://siteresources.worldbank.org/INTYTOYCOMMUNITY/Resources/Samuel_Freije_World_Development_Report_WBG.pdf, downloaded 5 May 2012.

Geldenhuys, J P. "Equity in health care finance after the abolishment of user fees: the experience of South Africa", Department of Economics, University of Free State, unpublished paper, undated – possibly 2008. Downloaded on 10 December 2011 from http://www.essa.org.za/download/2007conference/Geldenhuys_Equity%20in%20health.pdf

Gintis, Herbert and Samuel Bowles. *A Cooperative Species: Human Reciprocity and its Evolution*, Princeton: Princeton University Press, 2011.

Gordon, David. "Children, policy and social justice", in Craig *et al* (eds), 2008, pp.157-180.

Gordon, David and Shailen Nandy. "Measuring child poverty and deprivation", in Minujin and Nandy (eds), 2012, pp.57-101.

Green-Thompson, R W; T M Sibeko, and N C O Khaole. *National Task Team Report on Frere Hospital*, July 2007.

Gutiérrez, Francisco; Diana Buitrago; Andrea González; and Camila Lozano. *Measuring Poor State Performance: Problems, Perspectives and Paths Ahead*, Crisis States Research Centre Report, Instituto de Estudios Políticos y Relaciones Internacionales, London School of Economics and Political Science, 2011.

Hart, Julian Tudor. "The Inverse Care Law", *The Lancet*, February 1971, pp.405-412.

Holmqvist, Göran. "HIV and Income Inequality: If there is a link, what does it tell us?", Working Paper No. 54, Institute for Futures Studies, Stockholm and Nordic Africa Institute, Uppsala, April 2009.

Hoogeveen, Johannes G, and Berk Özler. *Not Separate, Not Equal: Poverty and Inequality in Post-Apartheid South Africa*, University of Michigan, William Davidson Institute Working Paper Number 739, January 2005.

Human Rights Watch. *Stop Making Excuses" Accountability for Maternal Health Care in South Africa*, New York: Human Rights Watch, 2011.

Joumard, I; C André, and C Nicq. "Health Care Systems: Efficiency and Institutions", *OECD Economics Department Working Papers*, No. 769, OECD Publishing. http://dx.doi.org/10.1787/5kmfp51f5f9t-en, 2010.

Joyce, Robert. "Poverty projections between 2010–11 and 2013–14: a post-Budget 2011 update, Institute for Fiscal Studies, Update to Brewer and Joyce (2010)". Downloaded from http://www.ifs.org.uk/docs/mimeo_rj_2011.pdf, 21 December 2011.

Kanbur, Ravi. "Poverty Disconnected", *Finance & Development*, December 2009, pp.32-34.

Kerr, Andrew and Martin Wittenberg. "The Impact of Changes in Statistics South Africa's Enumeration Practice on Average Household Size", unpublished paper, DataFirst, University of Cape Town. March 2012.

Klasen, Stephan. "Measuring Poverty and Deprivation in South Africa", *Review of Income and Wealth*, Series 46, No.1, March 2000, pp.33-58.

Kurukulasuriya, Sharmila. "HDR Impacts on PEOPLE'S Lives", PowerPoint presentation at HDRO/RBA Regional Technical Workshop on Measuring Human Development, Nairobi – September – 2007. Downloaded on 15 February 2012 from http://www.authorstream.com/Presentation/aSGuest492-92602-impacts-hdr-human-life-sharmila-news-reports-ppt-powerpoint/.

Labadarios, D; R Swart; E M Maunder; H S Kruger; G J Gericke; P M Kuzwayo; P R Ntsie; N P Steyn; I Schloss; M A Dhansay; P L Jooste; A Dannhauser; J H Nel; D Molefe, and T J vW Kotze. *The National Food Consumption Survey: Fortification Baseline (NFCS-FB-I): South Africa, 2005*, Pretoria: Department of Health, Directorate: Nutrition, 2007. Referred to as Labadarios *et al*, 2008.

Leamer, Edward E. "Sensitivity analyses would help", *American Economic Review*, Vol. 75, No. 3, 1985, pp.308-313.

Leibbrandt, M; Ingrid Woolard; Arden Finn, and Jonathan Argent. "Trends in South African Income Distribution and Poverty since the Fall of Apartheid", *OECD Social, Employment and Migration Working Papers*, No. 101, OECD Publishing. doi: 10.1787/5kmms0t7p1ms-en, 2010.

Leibbrandt, M; E Wegner, and A Finn. "The Policies for Reducing Income Inequality and Poverty in South Africa", Southern Africa Labour and Development Research Unit Working Paper Number 64. Cape Town: SALDRU, University of Cape Town, 2011.

Lorgelly, Paula K; Kenny D Lawson; Elisabeth A L Fenwick; and Andrew H Briggs. "Outcome Measurement in Economic Evaluations of Public Health Interventions: a Role for the Capability Approach?", *International Journal of Environmental Research and Public Health*, 2010, Vol. 7, pp.2274-2289.

Marzo, Federica, and Fabrice Murtin. "HIV/AIDS and Poverty in South Africa : A Bayesian Estimation", Groupe de Recherche en Économie et Développement International (GRÉDI) Working Paper 07-08, Université de Sherbrooke, Quebec, March 2007.

Maughan-Brown, Brendan. "Changes in HIV-related stigma among young adults in Cape Town, South Africa", Centre for Social Science Research, University of Cape Town, CSSR Working Paper No. 242, March 2009.

McCarthy, Paul. Extrapolating PPPs and comparing ICP benchmark results, International Comparison Program, 6th Technical Advisory Group Meeting October 3-4, 2011 Washington DC.

McKerrow, Neil and Mphele Mulaudzi. "Child Mortality in South Africa: Using Existing Data", in *South African Health Review 2010*, Durban: Health Systems Trust, December 2010, pp.59-72.

McLennan, D; H Barnes; M Noble; J Davies; E Garratt, and C Dibben. *The English Indices of Deprivation 2010*, London: Department for Communities and Local Government, 2011.

Metcalfe, Mary. *Commission Report: Verification of textbooks deliveries in Limpopo (July 2012)*, commissioned by the NGO Section 27, and the Department of Basic Education, 2012.

Meth, Charles. "Half measures revisited: The ANC's unemployment and poverty reduction goals", in Bhorat and Kanbur (eds), 2006, pp.366-458.

Meth, Charles. "Income poverty in 2004: A second encounter with the recent van der Berg *et al* figures", Working Paper No. 47, School of Development Studies, University of KwaZulu-Natal, September 2006.

Meth, Charles. "Flogging a dead horse: Attempts by van der Berg *et al* to measure changes in poverty and inequality", SALDRU Working Paper No 11, December 2007a.

Meth, Charles. " 'A world in one country': Poverty, extreme inequality, falling life expectancy and South Africa's Human Development Index (HDI)", unpublished paper commissioned by Statistician-General, South Africa, July 2007b.

Meth, Charles. "What is pro-poor growth? What are some of the things that hinder its achievement in South Africa?", paper commissioned by Oxfam. Delivered at NEDLAC Community Constituency Conference, Durban, May 2007c. e-published at http://www.oxfam.org.uk/resources/countries/downloads/research_reports_may07.pdf

Meth, Charles. "Sticking to the facts: Official and unofficial stories about poverty and unemployment in South Africa", DPRU Working Paper 07/123, Development Policy Research Unit, School of Economics, University of Cape Town, June 2007d.

Meth, Charles. *Social income in South Africa, an economy marred by high unemployment, poverty and extreme inequality*, Pretoria: HSRC, April 2008.

Meth, Charles. "Unemployment and poverty halved by 2014?", Working Paper No. 56, School of Development Studies, University of KwaZulu-Natal, December 2009.

Meth, Charles. "What do we know? Professor Servaas van der Berg's poverty estimates", Research Report No. 85, School of Development Studies, University of KwaZulu-Natal, November 2010a.

Meth, Charles. " 'Active' Labour Market Policies: Lessons for South Africa?", Research Report No. 86, School of Development Studies, University of KwaZulu-Natal, November 2010b.

Meth, Charles. "How not to present poverty research results: The South African case", SALDRU Working Paper 61, Southern African Labour and Development Research Unit, University of Cape Town, June 2011.

Ministry of Rural Development. *Report of the Expert Group to advise the Ministry of Rural Development on the methodology for conducting the Below Poverty Line (BPL) Census for the 11th Five Year Plan*, Government of India, New Delhi, August 2009. (Saxena Report, referred to as MRD, 2009).

Minujin, Alberto and Shailen Nandy (eds). *Global child poverty and well-being: Measurement, concepts, policy and action*, Bristol: The Policy Press, 2012.

Mullis, Ina V S; Michael O Martin; Eugenio J Gonzalez, and Steven J Chrostowski. *TIMSS 2003 International Mathematics Report*, Chestnut Hill, MA: TIMSS & PIRLS International Study Center, 2004.

Mullis, Ina V S; Michael O Martin; Ann M Kennedy, and Pierre Foy. *Progress in International Reading Literacy Study: PIRLS*, Chestnut Hill, MA: TIMSS & PIRLS International Study Center, 2007.

Musgrave, Richard A, and Peggy Boswell Musgrave. *Public Finance in Theory and Practice*, McGraw-Hill, 1973.

Mutasa, George. "The Disincentive Effects of Disability Grant on Labour Supply in South Africa: A Cohort Analysis", unpublished paper, Development Policy Research Unit (DPRU), School of Economics, University of Cape Town, March 2010.

Naidoo, Arulsivanathan Ganas Varadappa. *A Multi-Dimensional Measure of Poverty in South Africa*, unpublished PhD dissertation, University of Pretoria, 2007.

National Agricultural Marketing Council. *The South African Food Cost Review: 2006*, Pretoria: National Agricultural Marketing Council (and Department of Agriculture), 2006. Referred to as NAMC, 2006.

National Treasury and Statistics South Africa. "A national poverty line for South Africa", 21 February 2007. Downloaded from http://www.treasury.gov.za, 12 December 2011. Referred to as National Treasury, 2007.

National Treasury. *Estimates of National Expenditure 2009*, Pretoria: National Treasury, 11 February 2009. Referred to as National Treasury, 2009.

National Planning Commission. *National Development Plan: Vision for 2030*, Pretoria: National Planning Commission, RP 270/2011. Referred to as NPC, 2011.

Nicol, Edward and Debbie Bradshaw. "Maternal, Newborn and Child Survival: data challenges", in *South African Health Review 2010*, Durban: Health Systems Trust, December 2010, pp.73-78.

Noble, M; M Babita; H Barnes; C Dibben; W Magasela; S Noble;P Ntshongwana; H Phillips; S Rama; B Roberts; G Wright, and S Zungu. *The Provincial Indices of Multiple Deprivation for South Africa 2001*, University of Oxford, 2006a.

Noble, M; M Babita; H Barnes; C Dibben; W Magasela; S Noble; P Ntshongwana; H Phillips; S Rama; B Roberts; G Wright, and S Zungu. *The Provincial Indices of Multiple Deprivation for South Africa 2001: Technical Report*, University of Oxford, 2006b.

Noble, M; H Barnes; G Wright; D McLennan; D Avenell; A Whitworth, and B Roberts. *The South African Index of Multiple Deprivation 2001 at Datazone Level*, Pretoria: Department of Social Development, 2009.

Noble, Michael; Christopher Dibben, and Gemma Wright. *The South African Index of Multiple Deprivation 2007 at Datazone level (modelled)*, Pretoria: Department of Social Development, 2010.

OECD. *Reviews of National Policies for Education – South Africa*, Paris: OECD Publishing, 2008.

Planning Commission. *Report of the Expert Group to Review the Methodology for Estimation of Poverty*, Government of India, New Delhi, November 2009. (The Tendulkar Committee Report, referred to as PC, 2009).

Planning Commission. *Press Note on Poverty Estimates*, Government of India, New Delhi, January 2011. Referred to as PC, 2011.

Posel, Dorrit. "Self-assessed well-being: Analysis of the NIDS Wave 1 and 2 Datasets", SALDRU Working Paper 79, Southern African Labour and Development Research Unit; NIDS Discussion Paper 2012/2 (National Income Dynamics Survey), University of Cape Town, June 2011.

Ravallion, Martin. "How Not to Count the Poor? A Reply to Reddy and Pogge", unpublished mimeo, World Bank, 2002.

Ravallion, Martin. "Mashup Indices of Development", World Bank Policy Research Working Paper 5432, September 2010.

Ravallion, Martin. "On Multidimensional Indices of Poverty", World Bank Policy Research Working Paper 5580, February 2011.

Reddy, Sanjay G, and Thomas W Pogge. "How *Not* To Count The Poor", Columbia University, Version 6.2.3, October 29th, 2005.

Reddy, Sanjay G. "The New Global Poverty Estimates – Digging Deeper into a Hole", *Poverty Centre International: One pager*, September, 2008 Number 65.

Reddy, Vijay with contributions from **Anil Kanjee; Gerda Diedericks, and Lolita Winnaar**. *Mathematics and Science Achievements at South African Schools in TIMSS 2003*, Cape Town: HSRC Press, 2006.

Rehle, Thomas; Olive Shisana; Victoria Pillay; Khangelani Zuma; Adrian Puren, and Warren Parker. "National HIV incidence measures – new insights into the South African epidemic", *South African Medical Journal*, March 2007, Vol. 97, No. 3, pp.194–199.

Rehle, Thomas; Leickness Simbayi; Suzan Leclerc-Madlala; Olive Shisana; Nompumelelo Zungu; John Seager and Karl Peltzer. "HIV/AIDS and Society", monograph, Pretoria: Human Sciences Research Council, 2008.

Rehle, Thomas and Olive Shisana. "National population-based HIV surveys – the method of choice for measuring the HIV epidemic", *South African Medical Journal*, September 2009, Vol. 99, No. 9, pp.633-637.

Rice, Nigel; Silvana Robone, and Peter Smith. "Analysis of the Validity of the Vignette Approach to Correct for Heterogeneity in Reporting Health System Responsiveness", Health, Econometrics and Data Group, University of York, HEDG Working Paper 09/28, August 2009.

Saisana, M and S Tarantola. "State-of-the-art Report on Current Methodologies and Practices for Composite Indicator Development", European Commission Joint Research Centre and Institute for the Protection and Security of the Citizen, Italy, 2002. Cited in Joumard *et al*, 2011.

Saith, Ashwani. "Poverty-Lines versus the Poor: Method versus Meaning", Institute of Social Studies, The Hague, Working Paper Series No. 420, December 2005.

Sartorius, Benn K D; Kurt Sartorius; Tobias F Chirwa, and Sharon Fonn. "Infant mortality in South Africa - distribution, associations and policy implications, 2007: an ecological spatial analysis", *International Journal of Health Geographics*, 2011, Vol. 10, No. 61, pp.1-13.

Schneider, Aaron and Goldfrank, Ben. "Budgets and ballots in Brazil: participatory budgeting from the city to the state", Institute of Development Studies, IDS Working Paper 149, January 2002.

Schwab, Klaus and Xavier Sala-i-Martin (eds). *The Global Competitiveness Report 2011–2012*, Geneva: World Economic Forum, 2011.

Shah, Anwar (ed). *Participatory Budgeting*, Public Sector Governance and Accountability Series, Washington DC: The World Bank, 2007.

Shepherd, Debra L. "Constraints to school effectiveness: what prevents poor schools from delivering results?", Stellenbosch Economic Working Papers: 05/11, Bureau for Economic Research, University of Stellenbosch, 2011.

Shisana, Olive and Leickness Simbayi (eds). *Nelson Mandela HSRC Study of HIV/AIDS: South African national HIV prevalence, behavioural risks and mass media. Household survey 2002*, Cape Town: HSRC, 2002. Referred to as Shisana and Simbayi *et al*, 2002.

Shisana, Olive; T Rehle; L C Simbayi; W Parker; K Zuma; A Bhana; C Connolly; S Jooste; V Pillay *et al*. *South African National HIV prevalence, HIV Incidence, Behaviour and Communication Survey, 2005*, Cape Town: HSRC Press, 2005. Referred to as Shisana *et al*, 2005.

Shisana, Olive; T Rehle; L C Simbayi; K Zuma; S Jooste; V Pillay-van-Wyk; N Mbelle; J van Zyl; W Parker; N P Zungu; S Pezi and the SABSSM Implementation Team. *South African national HIV prevalence, incidence, behaviour and communication survey 2008: A turning tide among teenagers*, Cape Town: HSRC Press, 2009. Referred to as Shisana *et al*, 2009.

Silva-Leander, Sebastian. "On the Possibility of Measuring Freedom: A Kantian Perspective", Oxford Poverty & Human Development Initiative (OPHI) Working Paper No. 49, November 2011.

Smith, Peter (ed). *Measuring Up: Improving Health System Performance in OECD Countries*, Paris: OECD, 2002.

Smith, Peter. "Developing Composite Indicators for Assessing Health System Efficiency", in Smith (ed), 2002, pp.295-318.

Spaull, Nic. A Preliminary Analysis of SACMEQ III South Africa, Stellenbosch Economic Working Papers: 11/11, Department of Economics, University Of Stellenbosch, 2011.

South African National AIDS Council. *National Strategic Plan for HIV and AIDS, STIs and TB, 2012-2016: Draft Zero for Consultation*, Pretoria: SANAC, 5 August 2011.

Statistics South Africa. *Income and expenditure of households 2000 South Africa*, Statistical release P0111, 13 November October 2002, Pretoria: Statistics South Africa. Referred to as Stats SA, 2002.

Statistics South Africa. *Community Survey, 2007 (Revised version)*, Statistical release P0301, 24 October 2007, Pretoria: Statistics South Africa. Referred to as Stats SA, 2007.

Statistics South Africa. *Income and expenditure of households 2005/2006: Analysis of results*, Report No. 01-00-01, Pretoria: Statistics South Africa, 2008. Referred to as Stats SA, 2008.

Statistics South Africa. *Census Undercount and strategies*, Pretoria: Statistics South Africa. Undated, file created October 2010. Referred to as Stats SA, 2010.

Statistics South Africa. *Millennium Development Goals: Country Report 2010*, Pretoria: Statistics South Africa, 2011? Referred to as Stats SA, 2011a.

Statistics South Africa. *Living Conditions of Households in SA 2008/2009*, Pretoria: Statistics South Africa, Statistical release P0310, 15 September 2011. Referred to as Stats SA, 2011b.

Statistics South Africa. *Mid-year population estimates*, Pretoria: Statistics South Africa, Statistical release P0302, 27 July 2011. Referred to as Stats SA, 2011c.

Statistics South Africa. *Mortality and causes of death in South Africa, 2009: Findings from death notification*, Pretoria: Statistics South Africa, Statistical release P0309.3, 30 November 2011. Referred to as Stats SA, 2011d.

Swart, Rina; David Sanders, and Milla McLachlan. "Nutrition: A Primary Health Care Perspective", *South African Health Review, 2008*, Chapter 9, pp.129-147. Durban: Health Systems Trust, 2008. Referred to as Swart *et al*, 2008.

Taffesse, Alemayehu Seyoum. Comment on Alkire (2011), in Aglietta *et al*, 2011, pp.91-95.

Teschl, Miriam and Flavio Comim. "Adaptive Preferences and Capabilities: Some Preliminary Conceptual Explorations", *Review of Social Economy*, 2005, Vol. 63, Issue 2, pp.229-247.

Tladi, H S. "Poverty and HIV/AIDS in South Africa: an empirical contribution", *Journal of Social Aspects of HIV/AIDS*, May 2006, Vol. 3, No 1, pp.369-381.

Thurlow, James; Gavin George, and Jeff Gow. "HIV/AIDS, Growth and Poverty in KwaZulu-Natal and South Africa: Integrating Firm-Level Surveys with Demographic and Economy-wide Modeling", IFPRI Discussion Paper 00864, International Food Policy Research Institute, May 2009.

United Nations Development Programme (UNDP). *Human Development Report 1993*, New York: Oxford University Press, 1993.

United Nations Development Programme (UNDP). *Human Development Report 1999*, New York: Oxford University Press, November 1999.

United Nations Development Programme (UNDP). *Human Development Report 2001: Making New Technologies Work for Human Development*, New York: Oxford University Press, 2001.

United Nations Development Programme (UNDP). *South Africa Human Development Report 2003. The Challenge of Sustainable Development in South Africa: Unlocking People's Creativity*, New York: Oxford University Press, 2006? Referred to as UNDP, 2003.

United Nations Development Programme (UNDP). *Human Development Report 2005: International cooperation at a crossroads*, New York: Oxford University Press, 2005. Referred to as UNDP, 2005.

United Nations Development Programme (UNDP). *Human Development Report 2007/2008: Fighting climate change: Human solidarity in a divided world*, New York: Basingstoke: Palgrave MacMillan, 2007. Referred to as UNDP, 2007.

United Nations Development Programme (UNDP). *Human Development Report 2010, 20th Anniversary Edition: The Real Wealth of Nations: Pathways to Human Development*, Houndmills, Basingstoke: Palgrave MacMillan, November 2010. Referred to as UNDP, 2010.

United Nations Development Programme (UNDP). *Human Development Report 2011. Sustainability and Equity: A Better Future for All*, Houndmills, Basingstoke: Palgrave MacMillan, 2011. Referred to as UNDP, 2011.

Üstün, T. Bedirha; Somnath Chatterji; Maria Villanueva, Lydia Bendib; Can Çelik; Ritu Sadana; Nicole Valentine; Juan Ortiz; Ajay Tandon; Joshua Salomon; Yang Cao; Xie Wan Jun; Emre Özaltin; Colin Mathers, and Christopher J L Murray. "WHO Multi-country Survey Study on Health and Responsiveness 2000-2001", World Health Organisation, GPE Discussion Paper 37, 30 November 2001.

van der Berg, Servaas; Cobus Burger; Ronelle Burger; Mia de Vos; Gideon du Rand; Martin Gustafsson; Eldridge Moses; Debra Shepherd; Nicholas Spaull; Stephen Taylor; Hendrik van Broekhuizen, and Dieter von Fintel. *Low Quality Education as a poverty trap*, University of Stellenbosch, March 2011. Referred to as van der Berg *et al*, 2011.

Vandermoortele, Jan. "Equity begins with children", in Minujin and Nandy (eds), 2012, pp.39-53.

Vass, J. "A Review of Labour Markets in South Africa: The Impact of HIV/AIDS on the labour market", Employment and Economic Policy Research Programme, Cape Town: Human Sciences Research Council, 2005.

Wilson, E O. *On Human Nature*, Harmondsworth: Penguin (1978, 2001).

Wood, Claudia; Jo Salter; Gareth Morrell; Matt Barnes; Ally Paget and Duncan O'Leary. *Poverty in Perspective*, London: Demos, November 2012.

World Bank. *Global Purchasing Power Parities and Real Expenditures: 2005 International Comparison Program*, Washington, DC: The World Bank, 2008.

World Health Organisation (WHO). *The World Health Survey (WHS): Sampling Guidelines for Participating Countries*, Geneva: World Health Organisation. Referred to as WHO 2002a.

World Health Organisation (WHO). *World Health Survey (WHS) 2003: B-Individual Questionnaire*, Geneva: World Health Organisation. Referred to WHO 2002b.

World Health Organisation (WHO). *World Health Survey 2003, Report of South Africa*, Geneva: World Health Organisation. Referred to as WHO 2003.

Wright, Gemma, and Noble, Michael. *The South African Index of Multiple Deprivation 2007 at Municipality Level*, Department of Social Development, September 2009.

Appendix 1. NPC view on challenges in health and education

Extracts from the National Planning Commission's Vision 2030 on the challenges facing the health and education sectors.

Education: The Challenge

Although progress has been made in all subsectors of the education and training system, there are severe problems that must be solved to achieve the vision for education, training and innovation.

Early childhood development

Many South African children grow up lacking food and nutrition, which does not provide a good platform for cognitive development and full participation in society. Nowhere is this more evident than in South Africa's poor schooling outcomes and low skills base.

Children in the 0-4 age group have the highest mortality rates in the South African population and unacceptably high levels of stunting and exposure to violence and neglect. South Africa is also one of the 20 countries with the highest burden of under-nutrition. There are 2.8 million households and 11.5 million individuals who are vulnerable to hunger, over 72 percent of whom live in rural areas.

An average South African eats less than four out of nine food groups against the dietary diversity norm of seven out of nine. Children, pregnant and breastfeeding women and those living tuberculosis and HIV/AIDS are most at risk. Nationally, stunting affects almost one in five children (18 per cent), with higher levels in rural areas (24.5 percent), and urban informal areas (18.5 percent). About one in ten children are underweight, reflecting the severity of child under-nutrition. Micronutrient deficiency is also a problem. One woman in four lacks vitamin A and about a third of women and children are iron deficient. A third of preschool children are vitamin A deficient, 21.4 percent are anaemic and 5 percent suffer from iron-deficiency anaemia.

Access to early childhood development centres remains low. In 2009 about a quarter of children aged two attended early childhood development centres compared to nearly 60 percent of those aged four.

Schooling

Despite many positive changes since 1994, the legacy of low-quality education in historically disadvantaged parts of the school system persists. This seriously hampers the education system's ability to provide a way out of poverty for poor children. The grade promotion of learners who are not ready in the primary and early secondary phases leads to substantial dropout before the standardised matric examination.

In the Southern and East African Consortium for Monitoring Educational Quality III (2007) survey of grade 6 mathematics and reading, South Africa performed below most African countries. An alarmingly high proportion of grade 6 learners had not mastered even the most basic reading and numeracy skills. Of the 15 countries in the study, South Africa had the third highest proportion of functionally illiterate learners (27 percent), and the fifth highest proportion of functionally innumerate learners (40 percent).

Most children are in the historically disadvantaged part of the education system, which still serves mainly black and coloured children. Learners in these schools typically exhibit low proficiency in reading, writing and numeracy. The schools that historically served white children produce educational achievement closer to the standards of developed countries. Literacy and numeracy testing within the National Schools Effectiveness Study demonstrates that grade 5 learners in historically black schools are performing considerably worse on than average than grade 3 learners in historically white schools.

Two factors are largely responsible for the failings of the school system. The primary cause is weak capacity throughout the civil service – teachers, principals and system-level officials, which results not only in poor schooling outcomes, but also breeds a lack of respect for government. The mirror image of this weakness in the technical core is a culture of patronage that permeates almost all areas of the civil service. Nepotism and the appointment of unsuitable personnel further weaken government capacity. (NPC, 2011, pp.269-270).

Health systems: The challenge

The overall performance of the health system since 1994 has been poor, despite the development of good policy and relatively high spending as a proportion of GDP. Services are fragmented between the public and private sectors, which serve 83 percent (41.7 million) and 17 percent (8.3 million) of the population respectively. Imbalances in spending between public and private sector have skewed the distribution of services, which has been detrimental to both sectors and has led to cost escalation. Evidence suggests multiple system failure across a range of programmes, including maternal and child health, HIV/AIDS, tuberculosis and others, with a devastating combined impact. At the heart of this failure is the inability to get primary health care and the district health system to function effectively.

The fundamental importance of full community participation and the role of civil society has been underplayed and the focus on "people first – Batho Pele" has diminished. The culture of valuing and respecting the expressed needs of communities has faded, replaced by a top-down approach. The health system is fractured, with pervasive disorder and multiple consequences: poor authority, feeble accountability, marginalisation of clinical processes and low staff morale. Centralised control has not worked because of a general lack of discipline, inappropriate functions, weak accountability, lack of adherence to policy, inadequate oversight, feeble institutional links between different levels of services (especially hospitals) and defensive health service levels increasingly protective of turf and budgets.

Good policies are frequently not implemented in remote health facilities and district facilities, partly due to weaknesses in the relationship between medical staff and their patients. The essential values of primary health care have either not been practiced or given low priority. Many health professionals have become less concerned about carrying out their responsibilities and duties to their patients, their profession and society, than about personal benefits such as pay and working conditions. Resources have been inequitably distributed and crises and curative services are responded to rather than prevented.

To address these issues, in 2009 the Department of Health recommitted itself to a revitalised primary health care approach based on a reinvigorated district health system.

A comprehensive health service requires that primary and district health systems are linked to regional and central hospitals. Given that the core business of the health sector is clinical services that are both preventative and curative, it is important to provide the necessary environment for this to take place. This means that the bureaucratic process needs to support the clinical process, and not operate at the expense of the clinical process as it does at the moment. The integrated management team should ideally be led by a practising clinician, particularly at the level of health care delivery. Critical to this management model is decentralisation of authority with enhanced budgetary control.

Social determinants and ecology

The weaknesses in South Africa's health system are exacerbated by the burden imposed by multiple epidemics of communicable and non-communicable diseases. Health and health services have been shaped by powerful historical and social forces, such as vast income inequalities, poverty, unemployment, racial and gender discrimination, the migrant labour system, the destruction of family life and extreme violence. Progressive policies were formulated in the first years of the democratic dispensation and the public health system was transformed into an integrated, comprehensive national health system. However, poor leadership, inconsistent management and inadequate capacity meant that implementation and health outcomes fell short of expectations. There was a misguided attempt to change everything simultaneously, when many aspects of the system were not faulty. There are crucial issues that have never been satisfactorily addressed, such as the substantial human resource crisis facing the health sector and massive unemployment. (NPC, 2011, pp.301-302).

Appendix 2. *The weakness of poverty measures in wealthy countries*

It is not only the MPI whose impact may be negligible – in the UK, a democratic state, knowledge about poverty is abundant[158] – so is poverty. Poverty statistics aplenty, widely disseminated, appear to have little effect on the ability or willingness of the state to halt the steady increase in the number of people slipping below the poverty line (from about 12 million in 2004 to 13.5 million in 2008/2009).[159] Projections from the Institute for Fiscal Studies (IFS) micro-simulation model have absolute poverty among children and working-age adults rising from 13.5 million in 2008 to 16.5 million in 2013 (Joyce, 2011, p.3). The number of children in poverty rises from 2.6 million in 2008 (and 2010) to 3.1 million in 2013. The poverty line used is 60 per cent of real median income in 2010.[160] Much more elaborate than the MDGs, the UK Child Poverty Act of 2010 stipulates a (rolling) set of targets to be met. One of them, the absolute low income target for 2010, called for the poverty headcount among children to be reduced to 1.7 million, apparently using similar income criteria to those used by the IFS.[161]

In response to the 'policy relevant' material recited above, the Prime Minister chose to dispute the IFS projections, bolstered no doubt by a Treasury estimate of a drop of

---

[158] Enough is known about the matter to enable researchers to narrow the origins of about 60 per cent of the participants in the August 2011 riots to the 20 most deprived regions in the UK. See the article "Rioters were 'unruly mob' claims Theresa May", by Alexandra Topping in *The Guardian*, 18 December 2011.

[159] These figures are from The Poverty Site (http://www.poverty.org.uk/summary/key%20facts.shtml), accessed 20 December 2011.

[160] The IFS figures are readily available. They are reproduced on the websites of institutions such the Child Poverty Action Group (CPAG) – see, for example, the chart headed 'How many children live in poverty?' in the 'Facts & figures' section on the CPAG website (http://www.cpag.org.uk/povertyfacts/index.htm), accessed 20 December 2011. Absolute poverty measures appear in two forms – income before housing costs are deducted and income after housing costs have been deducted. The IFS figures cited above are compiled using the former, whereas the CPAG prefers the latter. The difference is not negligible – in 2009/2010, the latest year for which data are available, the proportion of children in poverty stood at 20 per cent before housing costs (2.6 million children), or about 28 per cent after housing costs (3.8 million children). Whatever the method chosen, the fact that in a country so wealthy, there are so many children in poor households is an obscenity. What makes it worse is that the problem is not primarily one of unemployment, or welfare dependence (that old bogeyman). According to the CPAG, "In 2009/10, 58 per cent of income-poor children were in households where one or more adult in the house was in work."

[161] See http://www.legislation.gov.uk/ukpga/2010/9/section/. Accessed 20 December 2011.

50 000 in the child poverty headcount over two years.[162] Asked during an interview with:

> "… ITV's *This Morning* [on 1 December 2011] about the news that 100,000 more children would be tipped below the poverty line by the measures announced in the Autumn statement… [delivered 29 November 2011]"

He said that:

> "I think there is a real problem with the way we measure child poverty in this country.[163] Because it's done on relative poverty, if you increase the pension, that means more children are in poverty. I think that's illogical. It's the right thing to do to increase the pension. It does not make any child in our country poorer, because you are giving pensioners more money at a time when they need it. I think what we have got to start doing is measuring how we help children out of poverty and keep them out of poverty."[164]

In making this sweeping assertion, Cameron ignored (i) the fact that the IFS poverty headcount estimates are prepared using both a relative measure (60 per cent of median income) and an absolute measure (60 per cent of median income in real terms in 2010), and (ii) that despite the 'generosity' to pensioners (allowing pensions to keep abreast of inflation), median income is predicted to fall (Brewer and Joyce, 2010, p.3).

As may be gathered from the origins of the comments offered above, this arms-length conversation took place between technical experts – a head of state briefed by a clever team from the Treasury, and a group of equally clever academic researchers.[165] England has a dense and talented network of poverty researchers; well-funded institutions like the Rowntree Foundation to stimulate, publish research and to publicise research findings, and a host of NGOs like the Child Poverty Action Group (CPAG) that articulate, to the best of their ability, what are believed to be the views of the poor. The collective voice of real living poor people is muted – almost

---

[162] This figure popped out of Treasury's attempt to model the impact of tax and welfare reforms introduced in the March 2011 Budget (Joyce, 2011, p.2).

[163] See 'Reality Check with Polly Curtis', "Is David Cameron Right to Dispute the Child Poverty Figures?", *The Guardian*, 1 December 2011.

[164] The initial set of measures proposed may be viewed in Annex A of government's 'New approach to child poverty' (DfWP and DfE, 2011, pp.68ff).

[165] At the University of Oxford, Cameron read Politics, Philosophy and Economics (PPE). His degree was awarded with first class honours. Robert Joyce of the IFS, also read for the PPE in the University of Oxford – the degree was also awarded with first class honours, while his MSc (Economics) from University College London was awarded with distinction.

nowhere to be heard. Ultimately dominating the conversation, because of the peculiarities of electoral law, is the minority group that presently holds power – it will be able (at least in the immediate future) to impose its view of the world.[166]

If knowledge (admittedly disputed) about the conditions of the poor does little to change policy in the UK, then it is likely that similar knowledge will have even less impact in the USA, if only because social protection is more threadbare in what is still, by far, the world's richest and most powerful country. Here is the most recent picture painted by the U.S Census Bureau:

- "The official poverty rate in 2010 was 15.1 percent — up from 14.3 percent in 2009. This was the third consecutive annual increase in the poverty rate. Since 2007, the poverty rate has increased by 2.6 percentage points, from 12.5 percent to 15.1 percent.
- In 2010, 46.2 million people were in poverty, up from 43.6 million in 2009—the fourth consecutive annual increase in the number of people in poverty.
- Between 2009 and 2010, the poverty rate increased for non-Hispanic Whites (from 9.4 percent to 9.9 percent), for Blacks (from 25.8 percent to 27.4 percent), and for Hispanics (from 25.3 percent to 26.6 percent). For Asians, the 2010 poverty rate (12.1 percent) was not statistically different from the 2009 poverty rate.
- The poverty rate in 2010 (15.1 percent) was the highest poverty rate since 1993 but was 7.3 percentage points lower than the poverty rate in 1959, the first year for which poverty estimates are available.
- The number of people in poverty in 2010 (46.2 million) is the largest number in the 52 years for which poverty estimates have been published.[167]
- Between 2009 and 2010, the poverty rate increased for children under age 18 (from 20.7 percent to 22.0 percent) and people aged 18 to 64 (from 12.9

---

[166] The nastiness of the Conservative Party knows no bounds, as attacks on the welfare state increase in ferocity. The hack (secretary of state) responsible for welfare recently plumbed new depths in an orgy of victim-blaming. See Polly Toynbee's opinion piece in *The Guardian* on 14 June 2012, headed "Iain Duncan Smith's fact-free dogma will make many more children poor". The strap says "I used to think the minister didn't understand poverty data. Now I think he knows the truth, but ignores it."

[167] As Ravi Kanbur has several times pointed out, when headcount poverty rates fall, but headcounts rise, one cannot say whether or not the situation has improved.

percent to 13.7 percent), but was not statistically different for people aged 65 and older (9.0 percent)".[168]

Apart from the mind-boggling magnitude of the numbers involved, the figures confirm what anyone with a nodding acquaintance with that great land would expect to discover about poverty, namely, that it is most severe among what used to be called minority groups (Blacks or African Americans and Hispanics, now on their way to becoming the majority). Also as one would expect, poverty rates among their children are even worse than they are among the groups as a whole, as Table 13 shows.

Table 13 Children Under 18 Living in Poverty, USA, 2010

Category	Number	Per cent
All children under 18	16 401 000	22.0
White only, non-Hispanic	5 002 000	12.4
Black	4 817 000	38.2
Hispanic	6 110 000	35.0
Asian	547 000	13.6
Source: U.S. Bureau of the Census, Income, Poverty, and Health Insurance Coverage in the United States: 2010, Report P60, n. 238, Table B-2, pp. 68-73. Downloaded from http://www.npc.umich.edu/poverty/ 20 December 2011		

Unlike the spurious objections to the UK poverty figures made by David Cameron, there are genuine grounds for engaging in debate about poverty measurement in the USA.[169] There are probably many ordinary people in the US who disagree with the

---

[168] Source: U.S. Census Bureau www.census.gov/hhes/www/poverty/about/overview/index.html, Downloaded 20 December 2011.

[169] An overview of the issues may be found on the website of the National Poverty Center in the University of Michigan, http://www.npc.umich.edu/poverty. Estimates using a revised measure have recently been published. These raise the overall poverty rate from 15.2 to 16.0 per cent, adding three million to the headcount. The poverty rate for children falls from 22.5 to 18 per cent, while that for the elderly rose from nine per cent to 15.9 per cent. Benefits from the USA's largest "anti-poverty program, Medicaid" are not treated as part of income, which causes poverty to be overstated somewhat. See the article by Dennis Cauchon "Debate brews over new method to measure poverty", in *USA TODAY*, 10

official statistics on poverty – prominent among them, one suspects, the many neo-liberal think-tanks in the country. Given generally conservative attitudes towards social protection, and given as well, the severely straitened economic circumstances in which the USA, along with many of the other members of the OECD club finds itself, it is unlikely that the country's meagre 'safety net' is about to become more generous.

If the estimates of the MPI in the USA for the over-19s in the year 2004, made by Alkire and Foster (2009) are anything to go by, then, for Hispanics especially, conditions are much worse than the income poverty measures would suggest – by their calculations, the headcount poverty using the traditional income measure was 22 per cent; that using the multi-dimensional approach was estimated to be 39 per cent (2009, pp.30ff). Under the conditions described above, however, it is hard to envisage how demonstrating this will have any positive impact at all on policy. Far easier to imagine, is an increase in the virulence of anti-immigrant sentiment.